Wisdom of tl

Wisdom of the Heart

Flora Perez

First edition
Published in Great Britain

By Mirage Publishing 2009

Text Copyright © Flora Perez 2009

First published in paperback 2009

A CIP catalogue record for this book
Is available from the British Library.

ISBN: 978-1-90257-845-3

Mirage Publishing
PO Box 161
Gateshead
NE8 4WW
Great Britain

Printed and bound in Great Britain by

Book Printing UK
Remus House, Coltsfoot Drive, Woodston, Peterborough, PE2 9JX

Cover image © Flora Perez
Layout by Artistic Director Sharon Anderson

Papers used in the production of this book are recycled,
thus reducing environmental depletion.

To my Family for their Love, Guidance and Support and a very special dedication to one of the most beautiful humans ever existed, for his Wisdom and for teaching us to have infinite Faith. I dedicate this book to you: Javier Wrtiz Nakach

Contents

Introduction

The wisdom of the universe has always been present in every one of us. It is in our hearts, just as our ancestors knew. We inherited from them their wisdom and experience for the path that the future society, the society of today, would take.

Unfortunately, we have taken a totally different path from the one of our original essence. Even if scientists and researchers have a theory that human beings, by nature, have within a violent instinct as well as their irrational and subconscious actions, the truth is that it carries something much purer in its essence and being.

By the hand of historians and interpreters, history has taught us that man's reality is the eternal struggle for what he wants, and that he has made his eagerness for excessive power, the pursuit of material wealth and control over all other, his main objective.

This is just a supposed reality of what is believed to be man's nature, and this only leaves us the option to justify our actions without love. It allows us to believe that it is part of the human and animal condition to obligate us to remain acting in a selfish and unconscious way, with which we only damage the environment and ourselves, as has been done until today.

Nevertheless, there have always been attempts to show us how wrong we are to think and act like this, because there have always been beings of great light who have never abandoned us. They have tried to let us know about their existence through small signals, which most of the time remained unnoticed or have not been

9

considered. Our history is full of these clear signals that have, as their main purpose, our acknowledgment and the true importance of what they are: treasures of wisdom of our wise people, who fought to leave us this sacred heritage. But, until today, we haven't known how to take advantage of it.

Without any doubt, we have ignored much of what would help us understand ourselves as persons and to understand what is around us. We are now entering a new stage for our planet and present society, in which we feel we have achieved much in scientific and technological terms. That's why it is necessary, more than ever, to know, with all our being, who we are and where we are going.

We have to recognise the importance and mission of what is around us which, without any doubt, would show us that the path we have taken is not appropriate for humanity or for the mission that each one of us have as beings of the universe. There is still some time left to acknowledge it and start repairing the wounds of what surrounds us, of our Mother Earth and, of course, of each living being.

Chapter 1

I Found a Friend

As I mentioned before, on our planet there have always been beings of great wisdom that have tried to help us find what we are looking for: Happiness. But happiness beyond the interpretation that each one of us has been given; I mean happiness in much more infinite terms, which are difficult for us humans to understand, because we have created and believed in limits for everything that is around us, starting with our own capabilities.

To be able to understand all which lies here, we need to open our hearts and minds a little more; we need to perceive, but above all to feel, what we have denied ourselves for so long, which is the presence of beings of great unconditional love that have given their lives for our well-being.

In my case, for a while I did not worry much about what I could not see or feel in my agitated, careless and selfish way of living. Sometimes, I became interested in learning a bit more about mystic themes, and I went to a Gnostic Centre. However, I only went a few times, because I could not be convinced about certain subjects. So taking into account my immaturity, being only seventeen at the time, you could say that this first approach to spirituality was not very successful.

However, life had a beautiful surprise for me, which would occur three years later at the time of the total eclipse of the sun on 11 July 1991. At the time I was twenty years old, and I was in a very good stage of my life. I felt 'good', but at the same time I felt lonely and empty, as though a part of me was lost. Even though I lived with my parents and my two sisters, and believed that I was reasonably 'happy', something inside me was feeling a certain nostalgia.

The eclipse was about to happen, and I really felt disconcerted by its great expectation, because people were very restless. I remember that, for some, the eclipse was a premonition of the end of the world or a great disaster. However, for others it was just a beautiful and natural phenomenon.

For me it was something unknown that I did not know how to describe. I did not feel anything unusual before it happened, although something disconcerted me, without knowing what it was exactly.

I remember when the eclipse began everything started to become dark; the dogs started barking and the roosters began to sing. I wanted to go out of the house, but my parents did not let me, fearing that I would look at the sun or that something dangerous would happen to me. Nevertheless, I went out to the courtyard where we had a big tree and I stood under it.

I felt so much happiness and emotion while observing the floor that was being clearly covered by half moons; it was like an act of magic of an unexplainable beauty. In that moment it seemed as though time had stopped - at least for me. I felt a great silence around me and it is something that is still hard for me to describe. It was a sensation of so much peace, happiness and emotion inside of me, that I remember I said with all the strength of my being: 'Oh god of mine, if my life or the life of others has to change, I ask you that it will be for the better…'

When I said this, I felt a great calmness, but at the same time I was really confused about what I felt, because normally I did not speak out in this way. I felt very happy, as if a huge weight had been taken off my being. It was very beautiful and was a sensation I could not understand, because never before had I felt so much intensity and love.

The next few days were different, because I felt a sensation of great happiness that I could not define, and I didn't know why. It was just as if life itself was trying to tell me that something magical and wonderful would come into my life, even though it was completely impossible to know that something like that would ever happen.

It was on 15 July around dawn. I was in a deep sleep when suddenly I began to feel as though someone had come into my bedroom and had switched on the light. I could clearly feel what I thought was the light of the lamp, so I just thought that my mother needed something and entered the room. But I was having such a pleasant sleep that I did not wake up completely. I felt that if I opened my eyes I would not be able to fall back asleep, so I did not want to pay too much attention to it and I waited for my 'mother' to leave the room.

However, the light was still there and I started to wake up. I decided to open my eyes to kindly tell my 'mother' to let me sleep. When I did that, a great radiance made me close my eyes and my heartbeat accelerated because, in that moment, I realised that my mother was not there.

A great feeling of anguish took over me and I did not want to open my eyes again, but at the end of my bed I felt a sense of warmth which overflowed me and disconcerted me even more. I could not speak; I tried but

I couldn't. I wanted to speak to my mother, wishing it was her that was there, but something told me that it was not like that. I don't know how much time passed before I decided to open my eyes again.

When I did so, I still could not fully appreciate what was there. However, when my eyes focused against the brilliant light before me, I could clearly see a very tall man. I immediately felt my heart accelerate like it had never done before and thousands of thoughts crossed my mind. The first and strongest one was that it was a burglar, and that he would hurt my family.

I closed my eyes again, wishing that he would disappear and that it was just part of my dream, but I still felt his presence. I know that some time went by, and I tried to be brave and open my eyes again. I was so scared and disconcerted, but I was finally able to open them again.

I was now able to see this man more clearly. He had the appearance of an old person, an oriental kind of face, and what appeared to be a little smile.

This really disconcerted me, because his appearance was not at all that of a thief or a bad person. There was also something about him that told me he would not hurt me.

I remember how the light was so bright and intense, but that the most surprising thing was to discover that it appeared to be coming out of the man's body. He seemed illuminated from inside and, at the same time, that light came out illuminating everything around him.

It was then, when he was just observing me, that he turned to his left and walked to the door of the room. I saw, as he walked away, that the white light went with him, leaving my room in complete darkness. I followed him with my eyes, and I could clearly see how he continued his way through to the living room, and there in the hall he disappeared out of sight.

This for me was something completely beyond any reasoning. I stayed in my bed for a long time without being able to talk or stand up until finally, trying to be brave, I went to my parents and told them, crying and astonished, what had happened.

My parents checked that everything in the house was in order and, as they did not find any evidence of someone entering the house, they considered that it had only been a dream. But for me, this experience was real, because I knew I was not sleeping. I could clearly remember what had happened. During the time that this experience lasted, even through my fear, I knew that what I was seeing was very real and could not be a dream.

During the following days, all my thoughts were about what had happened and I searched for an explanation. Although this explanation was never forthcoming, I was convinced that it had all been real. This certainty also made me reproach my cowardliness, for not having said a word to this person. I told myself a thousand times that, if it were to happen again, I would be brave and would speak to him, but I feared this would never happen.

So many questions went through my head without finding any answer. I thought that maybe it could have been a ghost, an angel, or just a product of my imagination, because I could not explain it. I tried to convince myself that perhaps it really had been a dream.

But I was not completely satisfied with this, because I knew that it *had* been real. I was sure it had not been a physical person, because it was impossible to get into our house without first running into my fierce dog, or leaving any trace of his visit.

15

Flora Rocha

Three nights after that experience, I went to the courtyard – where we had lots of big mango trees – to play with my dog. I used to go to this place to exercise and relax before going to bed.

While there, I started to feel a great uneasiness, equal to the sensation of being in a roller coaster. Immediately I connected this feeling – now I think I know why – with the experience I had lived three nights before. I knew that that same being or this person was there. My dog started to jump while looking to the back of the courtyard. Then I saw, at the bottom of the courtyard, behind a big tree, the same white and brilliant light.

The excitement and my heart could not wait. When I least expected it, I felt again this great nervousness and uncertainty. Suddenly I heard footsteps on the ground, and I saw how the silhouette of this person appeared and slowly came towards me. Although I could not see him very well, because of the great light I knew it was him.

Once again a thousand thoughts went through my head. I didn't know what to do, although I tried to tell myself that this was the opportunity to learn who he was and what he wanted. Then, when I saw that instead of showing aggressiveness, my dog calmed down and seemed to be behaving as though he was seeing a great friend, this reassured me.

Finally, he stood about two meters from me, with the same friendly smile as in our first encounter. I remember I perceived a beautiful aroma that I did not relate to him at that moment, but that also helped me - in a certain way - to control my emotions.

I tried to speak but the only thing I could say was 'Who are you?' He answered me with a soft voice, difficult to describe.

'I am your friend, I wish you to consider me as a

friend…'

I did not know what to say. In that moment, I felt many confused emotions and sensations. I could not believe that after thinking, and maybe wishing, it so much, I was again facing this mysterious being.

He really amazed me. When he spoke I did not seem to hear his voice in my ears, but rather I heard it inside me. Nevertheless, he still moved his lips when he spoke. That surprised me a lot. I remember that he said something more but, because of my disconcertment and curiosity, I did not understand what he was trying to express.

He kept talking and asking completely normal questions, like you would ask any other person you had just met. That also surprised me, because I thought that I would be the one asking the questions; but he was the one asking them, in a very simple way.

He asked me how I felt about my life, to which I could only answer nervously: 'Good'. He asked me if I was happy at school, and how my family and friends were doing. I remember I felt that he was only asking me these questions so that I would not feel so nervous. However, my nervousness was stronger than me.

He stood there for some minutes, I do not know how many, but enough for me to see him better than the first time. I realised that he was a physical person and not just an apparition (as I started to think).

His presence was beautiful; he transmitted something so wonderful that it made me shiver, feel excitement, and want to cry. His eyes reflected a great love and peace; his delicate, long and beautiful hands moved with great subtleness. His outfit really surprised me; it was a big robe, in a colour very similar to blue, which barely touched the floor. He was wearing some kind of beautiful linen shoes, which had a very beautiful kind of embroidery and symbols. After observing this, he smiled and told me: 'We will see each other very soon…'

Smiling again, he caressed my dog, turned and went away, leaving me completely surprised, but with a great beautiful and happy sensation that I still cannot explain.

His visit was something magical, and it filled me with emotions that I had never felt. I wanted to cry out of happiness, to run and tell everybody around me what happened, although my uncertainty and doubts where still pulling me. However, the great joy and happiness I felt were strongest, maybe because I knew that I would see him again soon, and so it happened.

After this encounter, there were many more. At the beginning, they would normally take place in the quietest places I knew, like the courtyard of my house, the beach, the countryside; it did not matter if there were people around. The next few days for me were of great disconcertment but, at the same time, of great happiness. My family, however, were a bit worried about this mysterious 'gentleman' that, for me, slowly began to be a great friend. At that time, I still did not

Even though, in the beginning, my main wish was to know who he was and what he wanted, I only asked him for his name, and he told me that it would be difficult for me to pronounce it, but that I should pronounce it as well as I could. So I started calling him Nintan, which is somewhat similar to his real name. Then, as time went by, I just called him Nintancito, as a symbol of my affection.

Deep inside me, I knew that knowing everything about him would be something totally out of logic, at least for me. I was also afraid of losing his friendship and his company, which had become very important to me;

for the first time I felt peace, as well as happiness and love for every little thing and, above all, he taught me to cherish my family. He taught me all of this in just a few days.

This does not mean that he turned me into a saint or anything like that, but I could realise how blind and confused I was about life and about everything that surrounded me, starting with the career I had studied, namely Marine Biology. I understood that science only look at the physical part of things and their supposed origin, without being able to go beyond, to the essence and feeling of every being, organism or micro-organism. Understanding the beauty and essence of each living being was something I learned for the first time, and it was not at school, but by an old, beautiful man full of love.

When I could calm down and try to understand that this went beyond anything I knew, to be able to understand him I knew I had to remove the fear and enjoy the presence of this being that intrigued and comforted me at the same time. I knew that everything in him was totally different to what I could know, even when I tried to think and to convince myself that he was just an extravagant and different person. I knew that there was in him something much deeper and astonishing.

I remember that in our occasional encounters there was always a great teaching for me. During one of those occasions, when I was resting at the beach, he came and sat next to me. I looked around me - there were many people and it surprised me that only some turned with curiosity to see him, but without giving much importance. It amazed me that only a few people were curious about this presence and that others were completely indifferent.

I asked him: 'Why are there so few people that feel any curiosity about your presence, when it is so different to what is "normal"? Would it be that they want to be discrete or that only very few people can see it?'

I tried in a very subtle way to know more about him and to make sure that I was definitely seeing him, that it was not my imagination. He answered me – as if he had heard my intentions and thoughts – 'Leave your worries, I am as real as this beautiful sea; I am not a product of your mind, I am part of your heart and you are part of mine.'

Without any doubt his answer reassured me and I felt that he really was someone very important for me, even though I could not explain why. Time went by, and his presence became more frequent. We talked about anything and generally he would let me speak more. He told me how important it was that I could express my wishes, fears, happiness and emotions. This really helped me to understand a part of me that I ignored and also, undoubtedly, it taught me to reveal my feelings to myself.

In another encounter when I was in the city, he said to me 'What a beautiful sky, what a beautiful flower, and what a beautiful world! Do you think it is beautiful? Do you like this flower? Say it, because if you express in words the beauty of what is around you, you will be giving a gift of great energy of light to every thing that you admire. This way you will help it to preserve its beauty, giving motivation and strength to it. And at the same time, you will be helping your being and your heart, as you will receive what you give. That is why you should not keep the good feelings and thoughts of admiration and love just for you; express them, this Mother Earth needs them. Even if it is hard for you to believe that this is a way of helping her to relieve her pain, it is a reality that all beings of this Earth should remember and understand…'

In every meeting we had, I got what I called a great learning experience. By listening to the beautiful things that he said, made me feel a great happiness; yet at the same time disconcertment, because it was as if my eyes were opening for the first time after a long dream. His beautiful presence, his subtle, delicate and sweet way of observing and expressing the things of this world and universe, made me want to know more about his identity, and who he was. Nevertheless, I was afraid of his answer; I feared not being able to understand, so I preferred to keep his friendship and to ignore his origins.

Approximately three months went by like this, when suddenly, when we met again, he told me: 'Now you consider me as your friend, your heart said this to me, that is why I have to tell you everything about who I am. You have questioned yourself so many times, without asking me, and I know you did it trying to be respectful, and maybe also fearing you would not understand clearly. I thank you for wanting to know me without setting conditions. I am someone like you and any other person on this planet, even with my slightly different appearance. But the most important thing of all, is that you discovered that I am truly your friend. As my friend, you will understand everything and from now on you will listen, know and see.'

The revelation of our friendship

What followed was incredibly beautiful. Since then, I feel that my life has become a beautiful fairy-tale; it was something that I ignored for a long time, yet now I have finally been able to enter the wonderful reality of this planet and everything that surrounds us. Since then, I have travelled to many places throughout this beautiful Mother Earth, accompanied by beings of great love and wisdom, like Nintancito, for the purpose to know and continue with the wonderful experience which started at the time of the 1991 eclipse.

It has not been easy because, before, I had to learn or 'remember' – with their help – all those necessary things to be able to physically live together with them. For example, the heavy energy charge that we humans have because of our misunderstood emotions, egos and habits, far away from what is real and natural. All this was, and is, a process that takes a lot of my strength, because our habits and beliefs are so anchored in our being, that it is not easy to recognise all that makes us move away from who we really are.

The key is to identify what affects us and what surrounds us. Starting from this acknowledgement, we will feel more clearly what is inside us, what will help us to understand ourselves better, and to have the certainty to be doing what the heart asks us.

The beings I'm referring to, like Nintancito, are just our brothers, like all the other inhabitants of this beautiful Earth. I do not think it would be fair to call them 'extraterrestrial' beings, because I have never met anyone more harmonised, committed and respectful to this Mother Earth.

At first, it was really hard for me to understand and acknowledge what was happening, or the explanation and words of Nintancito when he revealed his identity. I felt that his words completely surpassed my ears and my brain; it was as if they were going through my being, getting into an unknown place where I had the capacity of being able to understand everything that he told me.

Wisdom of the Heart

My reaction was of great astonishment. I couldn't believe what he was telling me, yet I knew it was true. He told me he could not tell me everything, because words were not enough to express that, but slowly, day by day, I would understand more and, above all, the reason why.

He knew I had a thousand questions and doubts, but he told me that only time would give me each answer. He suggested to me that we continue with our friendship without changing anything. That the only purpose of what had happened was for me to recognise my being, my wisdom and my heart because, by knowing myself, I would know and understand everything else.

He told me that the path that belonged to each being was happiness, which is waiting for every person on this planet. When I asked him how I could find that path, he just answered with great tenderness that he would help me find it.

Our bond turned into a great and infinite honest friendship. After his revelation, things did not change much. I tried not to think too much about it. I was afraid I would not understand if I thought about it; I knew that only time would help me to understand what was happening, and so it did.

Now, after seventeen years of being together and having great experiences with these wise and loving beings, I think I have been able to understand something, maybe what is most important: their Mission and their Great Wisdom.

Through all these years, I have dedicated more than half of my time and strength to understand and acknowledge that which we, as the human race, have forgotten: our Reality and the Wisdom of our Hearts.

This has always been with the guidance and love of those very beautiful beings who, with great affection, I call Masters, even though they do not consider themselves as such.

There is so much that we, the human beings, have to learn from Them and, because of that, I consider them Masters for all the inhabitants of this Earth, although they insist that we are our own Masters and Guides, because in each one of us the Infinite Wisdom is found.

Chapter 2

The Importance of the Presence of The Masters

Today is the time for us to remember, once and for all, the reality of who we are and that we can return to our origin, to all what we have learned to ignore. We should know that what we have been taught to see is not only real, but that there is much more than what we can imagine. Even the most beautiful fantasy tales cannot compare to the beautiful truth that, up to this day, we humans have ignored.

Through centuries we have been taught to forget and to focus our senses on what limits us, and it diminishes us to become living beings with few emotions and many thoughts.

Most of the time these thoughts move us away from our inner selves, and fill us with confusion and all kind of questions. Some of us ask ourselves these questions; others ignore them and leave them in a corner of our being. We conform ourselves to never answer them, and we centre ourselves again in what we can 'understand'. But we know that, deep inside, we are leaving what is most important aside, while trying, at the same time, to ignore our beautiful nature and reality.

We believe that we know our past, who we are or the reason for what is around us, but we have not wanted to discover the truth. We have also invented many laws and standards that strongly limit the perception and the acknowledgment of what is real and all those things and beings that surround us, leading us to ignore what is ignored.

Machines can be programmed so that they can recognise certain types of things and if, in their programming, they find a new object, they immediately delete it from its processor for being an unknown entity; this way it becomes unrecognisable. Therefore, it is not real for the machines, even though it actually is. Unfortunately, this is what we humans have become during all this time. Our brain is programmed to recognise and see only what society has dictated to us. Originally we had all the information and there were no questions, at least none without answers. Our wisdom was infinite and so was our origin as universal beings.

But, how do we finally get to wake up from such a long and profound sleep? The only way would be to recognise that we have many questions, and to find the answers we need to open those senses of our being that we hardly use. The advantage is that we can count on something sacred that will be our main guide in our search: the Heart. We need to be open to all the possibilities, not just those that limit us as persons. Rather, we need to be open to those possibilities that teach every one of us that we are owners of our own wisdom and knowledge as beings of the infinite universe.

To recognise what we have ignored for so long will make us feel free as the real beings we are. There have already been many centuries of confusion, hate and despair, in which we have almost convinced ourselves that our world is only that what we, until today, are able to see; that our life is tied to suffering, without being able to do anything else, and that we should accept what has

Wisdom of the Heart

been given to us until now. We are also sure that our origin is derived from our ancestor's evil or disobedience, which has marked us as eternal sinners by our own father.

From that point on, it is easy to know how our life can be if, through time and different theories about it, it makes us believe that we deserve nothing and that if we want something we have to suffer to obtain it. This is the common belief of most of the people on this planet, and this has brought us to live in the confusion we are living today.

We have many questions and few answers, and we need to understand who we are, and how beautiful our creation is. We need to break with what they have tried to sell to us as reality for thousands of years; it is essential more than ever that we achieve this and, therefore, we need to recognise that we can understand and comprehend, what we may have denied, to consider as real. This is only possible by trying to feel more with the heart and to ask questions about ourselves and about what surrounds us.

There is a beautiful reality outside this world, which has taught us to create and to believe, and there is another reality that the great Masters of Love and Wisdom have been trying to rescue. That's why they have been fighting for so long, so that we do not forget it, and for that little light that still exists in our being to not be extinguished completely. Their fight has been of a total and unconditional dedication. It is a fight that has been ignored by many and changed by many others. However, this must change.

All of us, the inhabitants of this planet, have to know about those beautiful beings, that have given us so much for such a long time, and of whom we know so little, or nothing. Their fight is that of Love, giving an example for all of us living on this Mother Earth. A great Mission we cannot ignore.

The mission and help of the Masters on Earth

There are many theories regarding the origin of life on Earth but, even with all the assumptions and studies about life's source and development, scientists have not been able to agree on this. They have been trying to convince themselves that life on this planet came about probably by way of meteorites, charged with small particles, which developed under the right conditions. Some others do not even dare to assume that the 'seed' that originated life came from outer space, but that they consider it the result of a long and constant evolution process, which resulted in what we presently are.

Unfortunately, for scientists it is impossible to feel more than to think; their great mistake has been to try to find an answer to everything by science. They have wanted to discover and describe man as a machine, by seeing and considering only the material side while, in reality, we are much more than that. They have tried to explain life through genetic science, believing that they will find the answers to our origins and the reasons for our shortcomings and virtues. The answer is much simpler than we think, and it is inside each one of us.

Science has given us much in many respects; this cannot be denied nor forgotten. But it is impossible to find the answers that explain what surrounds us, because its main base is the rational part of each human being and that, unfortunately, is only the minimum part of what we are.

The origin of life is something so beautiful and wonderful that it seems as unexplainable as incomprehensible, at least in the way we see and explain life, because our limits prevent us from knowing the truth.

When I could know – but not fully understand – the origin of life on this Earth, I discovered how wrong we humans have been. The Masters' explanation was clear and simple and, because of its great importance and meaning, it is difficult for us to understand or to comprehend. That is why I consider it is very important for us to know the mission of these beautiful masters, because in this way we will know a bit more about ourselves.

Through Nintancito and other Masters, I began to learn in these seventeen years the great mission of help and love that they have given us since the beginning of the human race. The best way to know that beautiful mission has been by bonding together in a physical level with many of the Masters who have always been amongst us.

They have tried to avoid teaching me through words; rather, they have done it through their example, their work, and going directly to the sacred places on Earth where they live. They consider that all the actions of beings are the honest language of their spirit and, with this beautiful teaching, I have been able to discover their great honesty; above all, I have learned of their great infinite Love and Wisdom towards each living being of this planet.

Living with them has been something that has implied learning and to control my energy and. It was not easy at the beginning, to know that to be able to be physically close to other Masters I needed to learn to control the discharges of emotions, which are nothing more than energy generated by our body. The explanation is that most of the time these discharges are negative or dense, which have prevented us humans to see and feel the subtle things.

It was a long learning and discovering process. Finally, and with hard work, I managed at least to know a bit more about myself and to learn not to harm these beautiful beings with my emotions, thoughts and emotional discharges. It was not easy, because it took me about a year to achieve this and it would have taken a lot more had it not been for the love and patience of Nintancito.

This has allowed me until today to know closely their mission and way of life on this planet. That's why, with their permission and support, I will try to make their presence clear in this book, their mission and love to each inhabitant of this wonderful Earth; above all, to discover their reality, which breaks with the myth that our angels or beings of light are intangible and invisible to us.

The Masters' presence was documented and cherished by our ancestors, due to the great closeness they had with them. They never looked at them as different or as foreigners of this planet; on the contrary, they were always considered as great guides, wise people and brothers. They helped them to understand better the treasures that we posses as beings of this earth and the universe. For our ancestors, the Universe was part of everything. Their lives were centred on the stars because they knew they were connected to the cosmos, just like this Mother Earth.

Therefore, amongst our ancestors existed a conjugation which did not only implicate the need to watch the sky, but rather the communication with the stars and their inhabitants. For them, limits did not exist, and they knew that the destiny of their people and lives depended on the guidance of their own wisdom, which they considered was directly connected to the universe.

The humans of the past had a great wisdom. They were aware that their predecessors went through disasters, which caused their disappearance on earth, so the new generations tried to repair the past damage by connecting with their inner strength, which is the heart. The communication and bond with the Masters from different places of the universe was not impossible for them. On the contrary, it was something normal to expect the help and guidance of Elder Brothers, who would lead them to meet and to re-encounter the most sacred, which is: the Wisdom of the Heart.

When I could learn all of this with the Masters they told me that it was very curious that nowadays it was so difficult for us to believe that this bond with the universe was real, as to help and guide the people or planets is something that we humans still do. The example is that, in our world, there are missionary people who travel from one country to another to protect those who need it, irrespective of whether they belong to their country or to another one far away. That is exactly what happened for thousands of years on this planet, with Brothers, Masters, Friends, or however you want to call them, from beyond the stars, universal beings of great love and wisdom, who listened to our calls for help.

In the most ancient texts and engravings of different cultures, they clearly refer to the importance and transcendence that these Masters had in the development of the people; most of the time they were considered as 'gods' (although the nearest translation would be Guides or Brothers). They participated in a direct way with each person that tried to discover the most beautiful within their creation, which was that great force of love and wisdom that is found in the hearts. They lived with the people in a harmonious and respectful way. In this relationship, people could go within themselves and take an internal journey to their own nature; in this way they could discover their own god and their strength of wisdom to develop any activity related to the universal laws of Love and free will.

I want to make clear that their main mission has not been to manipulate us or to control our lives (like some people say), but rather to show us that we are capable of achieving ANYTHING as the universal creation that we are. Unfortunately, the great respect and love that our ancestors felt for their brothers and Masters has been greatly misunderstood, and we have come to consider this more as a worship, cult or fanaticism.

But the great contradiction of this theory begins by saying that the ancient cultures had extraordinary developments in different fields, advances that even for our time are remarkable and of an unequalled quality. At the same time, it is said that, in ancient civilizations, there were cruel and savage warriors, where the heritage to which we have access is of beings of complete evolution in every aspect. Their great respect, love for life and to all the elements of nature, speaks very clearly of their Great Spirit and wisdom.

This is the difference between us, the current humanity, and the one of the past; while they fought time after time not to lose contact with the most sacred, which was their Mother Earth and Cosmos, we fight day by day to move further away from them and, with our thoughts and actions, we destroy the most valuable that we have: Life.

Undoubtedly, the presence of the Universal Masters has been of great importance for all of us living here. This has been very difficult to accept, especially for the organisations that, in a certain way, control this world and its inhabitants. Even some have tried to hide their presence and to distort their mission.

For example, all those ancient codes or texts of different ancient cultures which could show us in a very evident way the presence of these Masters, have 'disappeared' and are kept in custody by people or organisations that which to hide what now is very evident: life on other planets and the great influence of love that They had in our history as humanity.

Those few records regarding this reality, which is still in everybody's reach, have been interpreted by 'experts', but they try to relate them as much as possible with what we are today as civilization. They show us that those societies were very similar to the ones of today, except that they were more savage and violent. With this they want to show that we have evolved as a society. However, this is not the case.

Discovering the true reality of our ancient people will, without any doubt, make us realise that we have lost much of our true identity, and of the great beauty of lives. That is one of the main reasons why these beautiful Masters are trying by different ways to communicate to us our own reality. It is today more than ever that we need their help and orientation to find that world that we have left in the past.

It is very important to recognise the Mission of these Masters, because they have done part of the work that we still have not been able to complete: not just to protect the earth and its nature, but mainly to give love to everybody. They live with us; many are friends or companions that do tasks as any other, but only with the intention of closeness, to fraternise, to feed us with Love. They try to give us energy which, in some way, will involve us and will help us to feel more joyful and happier. They know that this way we will involve our families, friends or neighbours with these feelings, which is one of the ways to help this Mother Earth.

Over the years I have met many of these Masters who fulfil different missions or works. Most of them remain unnoticed, even though their physical presence is a bit different to ours, but our current way of living is so accelerated and, at the same time, so blind that only occasionally can we centre our attention on beautiful things like them.

To know and understand the different ways in which they have helped was something that surprised me, because the things or situations that for us are of minor importance, for them represent a great responsibility. They consider that no small mission exists and that love and care should be the same for ALL, because everything is life and belongs to the one universe.

The lost civilizations

Much has been said and theorised about the age of the human being on earth. However, we have not been able to reach an exact conclusion because, when finally it seems possible to make a calculation, more evidence comes to light that brings down the previous one.

For the Masters, creation has no limits of any kind; the only ones that believe in them are us, its creators. Therefore, time is relative just like matter and, if we want to calculate something that does not fit within the created limits, it will be almost impossible for us to determine any of the great mysteries that are around us because they are events that surpass our limits.

We urgently need to do something, with all that limits

us, to live only as finite beings, when our reality is infinite. Ahead of us we have so much to discover, and we will be part of that beautiful reality, but in order for this to be possible it is necessary to break all the preconceived ideas that have taken us to believe in our current 'reality'.

For example, our planet is much older than previously believed until today and, therefore, life on it. Civilizations have disappeared without trace and because of that they have been ignored. Our current society was preceded by a great number of communities, which went through situations that took them to their total destruction. Our Aztecs, Mayans, Egyptians, Greeks, etc., clearly referred to past civilizations in their texts and archives, which disappeared due to various catastrophes and were reborn again with the few that survived such destructions.

Our American continent is where the most ancient civilizations on Earth were born. The traces of their cultures have been safeguarded in nature, thanks to the great wisdom of the people that came after them and who tried to save the heritage and wisdom of their ancestors.

Different American cultures all affirm that, in our Great Mother Earth, four great destructions occurred which had been announced by the 'gods' of the stars. Those cataclysmic events happened when the inhabitants – which defined the Earth's destiny - forgot that the base and centre of the 'Infinite Expression' was harmony which, in turn, was the bond between nature and men. This connected them with their essence: the universe.

Unfortunately, these civilizations that preceded our most ancient cultures came to have great achievements and success based only on power and control, slowly forgetting their true mission as humans and people. Their relationship with what surrounded them became more negative and destructive; they caused wars, violence, hunger, death and destruction. The communication with our brothers of nature became void, which led them to completely forget their true reality. In this way, they submerged slowly into darkness, which would lead them to their own destruction.

There were periods on Earth when man ceased beings the leader of this planet; he could not control anymore what he before considered his property. It was then that we asked our brothers of the stars again for help and guidance for the construction of new civilizations, based only on the first law of the universe: the Law of Love. They, as they had already done long before, answered our call with all of their conviction and faith in our need to find again our sacred path of happiness.

In this way, a great era of our planet started, in which the presence and company of our Masters would be determinant in recovering again the wisdom buried in a past and forgotten by the inhabitants of the Earth. Their bond and teaching initiated in us a search to find ourselves again as beings of great wisdom and to return to the more important of each one: the Wisdom of the Heart. That important help and relationship with our Masters – as I referred to before - was made clear by what we today call the great civilizations of the past.

The Egyptians are an example of these civilizations, which were in great darkness and confusion when their people disappeared. That's why they asked for help, love and guidance by the Masters; they knew that in this way they could reconstruct their life and have a new dawn for their people. Many Masters answered the calling, amongst them one that became one of their main Guides: Osiris. This being was a great Master that helped in a definite way the birth of what we today know as the great splendour of Egypt.

On the other side of the world, in Central America, the Master Quetzalcoatl was of great help and guidance to the different civilizations that lived in the region from Mexico to Honduras, where he was considered for many centuries as the guide and creator of wisdom and light of the civilization and its inhabitants. The Lord from Venus, Visitor from the Universe and Feathered Serpent are a few of the names that they gave him.

The representation of the feathered serpent was given because it was considered as the worldly and low of man, so that the feathers represented the eagle, the ascension and wisdom of the universe. This meant for them the evolution of man, who had lost his way but had finally managed to find it in his heart.

Throughout our planet's history there are endless examples of the Masters that have given their help and guidance; Quetzalcoatl and Osiris are only two of the most documented in history, and there is evident reference about their universal origin.

The work, dedication and love of these great beings has been clearly expressed in the great texts and monuments. However, their presence on this planet, most of the time, has been listed as mythical – what anthropologists use to justify the clear and real evidence of the presence of beings that have come from the universe. This is sad, because it has been slowly taking us away from reality and from our relationship with our brothers of the stars.

Maybe we are fearful of classifying these great 'gods' (Masters) as extraterrestrial beings, because of the negative interpretation of this 'phenomenon'.

That's why it is very important that we start

discovering the great heritage from the past and stop submitting ourselves with what society wants to impose. Any one of us, children of this Earth, can find and decode the answers and heritages from the past and present; but for that we first need to have enough love, and bring out the Wisdom of the Heart that for so long has remained asleep.

The presence of the Masters has been and is a great reality since time immemorial.

The universe and its visitors

The mission of the Masters on this planet is much more serious and beautiful than anyone could imagine. Much has been speculated regarding their clear presence on Earth, untrusting their intentions or simply comparing their motives with those of the humans who want to 'conquer' the universe. It is then necessary to become aware that we, the inhabitants of this planet, are in a stage of fallback as humans, regarding Love, compassion, humility, equality, and so many other forms of feeling and manifestation that we have almost lost completely.

Our motives for travelling to the Moon, Mars, or any other planet in this solar system are based on the 'education' of power and conquest learned by this society that takes, as a principle, dominion above all things.

To take advantage of the material resources of other planets, expand the territory and, consequently, power itself, are some of the many reasons for us humans to travel to space. However, these are our objectives due to the way of life we lead, but for the beings of other planets, that have felt and taken the law of Love as the foundation and purpose of life, it is completely absurd to think that their presence here is for material purposes, to conquer, for power or experimentation.

The human being is distrustful due to the information that has been inherited from generation to generation, and this has integrated into our own genes. We always believe that others want something from us. Since our childhood we have been taught to distrust. When we were born, we learned to distrust the arms that were not of our parents. That mistrust, which begins from birth, gets stronger over the years. It makes us live with a certain fear of being betrayed and thus forces us to cover ourselves with an emotional armour to protect ourselves against the 'aggression' of others.

This can help us to understand that, if we distrust our own humanity, which is ourselves, what could we expect from a humanity that comes from other planets? This is maybe one of the reasons why we deny the existence of beings from another world.

On the other hand, for those who do allow themselves to believe in Their presence, the reason for Their stay amongst us has made some people feel distrust towards them, believing them to be cold and horrible beings that just come to Earth to experiment on us and take our resources.

It is necessary to be honest about what is happening, of what surrounds us. Many years and periods have been of confusion and denial that have caused us to walk through life blindly. The presence of these beings and life from the universe is nothing compared to what we humans are; we are confused, or simply ignorant of what true Love is. The meaning of this word is limited by the 'human' language and, of course, by each person's actions.

It has been feared that beings from other planets are 'negative' or that their intentions are not good. However, it seems we have forgotten that evolution of humanity is evolution on all levels: scientific, philosophic, spiritual, etc. We humans apparently are in an ascendant state – at least on the scientific level – which is far away from reality, but we believe or try to convince ourselves that it is like that, when the truth is that our projects to travel into outer space are completely limited.

Man presumes to have reached the Moon, is trying to get to Mars and has had several space missions. However, the problems for the scientific man seem to become bigger and bigger. It has come to a point where our projects cannot be materialised - at least, not how we want; our efforts to study other planets' composition have been ruined without reaching our goal and the necessary results, which wrap us in circles, will only take us back to the beginning.

That is when many questions arise, such as: Why is it that we cannot advance further in order to reach other planets as we can travel to other countries? Can we humans really one day reach other planets in this solar system? Are we in all human aspects prepared for this?

Thanks to the Masters, I now understand that we humans are not yet ready to reach beyond our planet. We will be able to visit the boundary of Earth and try to reach her sister planets, but if our technology continues as it is, those 'dreams' of reaching other planets will remain a dream.

The truth is that the scientific community has separated from what is spiritual, without even considering that matter is not only matter and that inside it there is a beautiful potential which, until today, has been ignored. They have not wanted to realise that the more a being is capable of knowing itself and what is around it, the more capable it will be of reaching the most recondite places of its mind and spirit. This will be translated as the capacity to control, manage and understand through reason, the Mind-Heart, all that which technologically has still not been able to achieve.

The fact that we humans still have not been able to achieve travel through the universe and its planets is due to the laws that prevail in it, but above all the Law of Love. In these matters – unfortunately - we are in a backward position that prevents us from making these voyages, because our intentions are still very distant from being the best. While there is not a true feeling of Love and a clear purpose that is based on the laws of respect, harmony and, of course Love, it will be almost impossible to visit other planets, because the universal laws will prevent us from doing so.

We should remember that these laws do not only exist for us here on Earth, the universe also has its own laws although, of course, those laws are very different from ours, because their main basis is Love.

These Laws of Love and respect obviously apply for all manifestations of universal life; therefore it is practically impossible that 'negative' beings from other planets could come to our Planet Earth to harm us or to experiment on us. These same laws that stop us, because we are so far from love, also limit all those beings that are outside this first law, which is essential to break the time-matter barrier. Every being that comes from the universe should be, by law, a being of complete Wisdom, which has, as its foundation of life and force, Love and all that is derived from it.

I know it is a little difficult to understand that it is like this, when there are so many witnesses of abducted and tortured people under a supposed 'extraterrestrial' model.

All this information has helped us to move away and

to distrust, even more, what is reality and what is based on the history of our Earth. However, maybe that is the purpose, to move us away and scare us away from what really is a wonderful truth; for sure, it would give us the necessary strength to discover what has been hidden for thousands of years under names like Mythology and Fantasy.

That is why we need to open more our understanding, not only at a mind level, but also at a spiritual, heart and feeling level. In this way we will be able to connect and to use something that never should have been separated: the mind and the heart that, for so long, have been in competition.

There is no more evil than the one created by all those that got carried away by egos, actions which were totally distant from love and compassion. It is necessary to learn to protect ourselves from those 'invisible' enemies that most of the times are summoned by us with our actions of hate, anger, resentment, etc. We cannot let the opportunity to bond and feel something as wonderful as the reality of the Masters to get away; we have to fight to return to that natural state of cosmic bonding, as it is part of our creation as humans and it is fundamental in the eternal search for happiness.

The answers are found in the Heart, the source of all Wisdom: the eternal Infinite.

Chapter 3

The Masters and their Anecdotes of Love

Ever since the first moment of my relationship with Nintancito and the other Masters, I could immediately feel their great love emanating from their being. I remember many anecdotes and conversations that touched me very deeply and made me think about how far away we are from living in fullness and in real harmony; mainly, to understand that we humans show very little love and respect.

I was in Paris one afternoon, walking with Nintancito and three other Masters that live in the Himalayas; we were going to a very crowded place where there were people from different nationalities who were visiting a very ancient place full of energy from the past. The purpose of going to this place was to learn in which way the energy of places (most of all, the old ones) influence people's energy.

It was then that one of the visitors, who was admiring the beauty of the place, threw a little piece of wrapped paper on the floor. This made one of the lama Masters rush to this 'trash' and take it in his hands with such an incredible tenderness and affection. Then, he started speaking to the little wrapped paper and said in a soft voice: 'I thank you with all my being for the service you have given; you were and you are something important for all, and we thank you for the good you did for us. These are words of the person that forgot the importance of your essence, but inside of him, in his heart, his thankfulness is there.' Then he went to a trash container where he carefully deposited it, not without first thanking it again for its service.

This had a very strong impact on me. It is difficult to say with words, but I felt such a great happiness at seeing it and, at the same time, a great sadness; that great love and respect shown to the trash showed me that those feelings were not only for what we have been taught, but for everything that exists on this Earth.

From the Masters I have learned that life is EVERYTHING, because EVERYTHING is energy and energy is life, in different manifestations and forms, but still life. However, it seems that we have forgotten this fact, which is of vital importance for the harmony of ourselves and, therefore, for Earth.

When I had the chance I asked the Master why he behaved this way with the trash, because it really surprised me. He began to answer me with a big smile and so much love in his eyes that, before he even said a word, I started to cry.

He told me: 'Do not be afraid to discover that you have lost opportunities to love, let those tears come out because they want to tell you about the greatness of infinite love and the sadness when you try to limit it. Listen to your heart because he will tell you that you should never set limits for love because, like the universe, it is infinite, without limit, thus their creation and manifestation are this too. Everything that surrounds you is alive like you are and, like you, needs the love and affection of each being, of this beautiful Earth. Do not be afraid to discover this, on the contrary open your being and liberate Love, giving it to EVERYTHING, without limiting it to the form or manifestation. The more you do this the more you will discover the wonders that, until today, you have not been able to see and that are just waiting for all of you, the children of this Mother Earth.'

His words, but mainly his attitude, showed me the great love that emanated from his being for each thing, no matter what its form or size. It was something very hard to discover how the Masters have so much respect and love to ALL, and how it is that we 'humans' are not able to show and to say to our family, friends or neighbours: I love you.

It is very important and necessary to show affection towards each being, yet it seems we persist in forgetting this or just do not consider it. The lama Master, who had such a beautiful attitude, told me about the importance of Love and the manifestations of it, telling me: 'Our universe, the INFINITE EXPRESSION, is the manifestation of the sublime energy of Love; that beautiful essence is found in the Heart, the centre of force and light of each person; it vibrates and lives with such intensity inside each being, that it is necessary to manifest and give something of what we receive, to all our fellow creatures, and the equal of each being that inhabits the universe which is ALL that is around us.

'Each being,' he continued, 'as small or insignificant as it may appear, possesses the same as you, like me and anyone on this planet; it feels and vibrates the same way, so it's capable of suffering and enjoying like any human does. They have an unknown language for the majority, with which they communicate, transmitting only the great admiration and love that they feel for you, their big brothers. And as big brothers they are a great example for each living being of this Earth; animals, plants, minerals

45

and everything that is created after that. Do not be afraid to love without measure; if the universe is limitless, so is our capacity to love, and that Love will make you fulfil the most important mission: Being happy.'

Again, the words of this Master had a great impact on me. I had to take time to fully appreciate their meaning and to discover my great fear of love, and show that. I hope that they also have the same effect on each person that reads this.

The Love that these Masters feel for us is so strong that it is very difficult to be able to transmit, through words, something so sublime and beautiful; however, I hope that, through these anecdotes and attitudes of Love, we can comprehend and understand their mission and dedication for all the children of this Mother Earth, in a more profound way.

Marginalized and loneliness

One of so many experiences of great Wisdom and Love, which I had with these beautiful Masters, happened also in a European city, during a cold winter. Walking outside a big church with my husband and some Masters that accompanied us, I suddenly felt a great uneasiness and disconcertment. It was then that, far away, I could distinguish an old lady sitting on the sidewalk and reclining on one of the market stalls that were nearby; beside her was one of the Masters.

I saw how this Master was sitting beside her, taking her hands and kissing them. I wanted to get near to them to listen, so I asked the Masters that were beside me for their permission. Immediately they consented.

Then, I was able to hear and perceive that the old lady was sick, and I knew by her appearance that she lived on the streets. The Master, whose mission of Love consists on giving help, protection and guidance to women or to any living being, with infinite sweetness whispered in her ear how beautiful she was inside and outside, and how her presence had been of help to the city and the planet. His words, full of Love and light, made her realise that her life had not been worthless.

I remember that she said: 'Who are you? I do not know you, but I feel that you have always been here and that it has been impossible for me to meet you before. Why, if you are so clean and handsome, would you help a woman so dirty and ugly like me? Is it maybe that you are blind, or it is that you want to take away something from me when I die? No, your face is that of an angel and your eyes draw me away from fear and pain...'

The Master answered: 'Who I am is not important. I am here next to you and that is what should matter, because you opened the way for me to be together in this moment. That is why I am very happy and so you should be, for being such a beautiful woman and for have given so much to this Earth. I am not blind, and everything I am telling you is true as it is what I see in you; I would never take away anything from you although, giving it a second thought, yes, I would take away the pain if I could do it. But I thank you for calling me angel face, because I know what that means for you.

'It satisfies me much to know that your fear and pain have disappeared,' he continued, 'but I am not doing this, you are doing it, because you use your heart full of light and relief when you tell me these beautiful words. At the same time, you do it towards yourself, flooding yourself with peace and taking away the pain. Remember that you will always live, and that everything that you have lived through has had a reason; your existence has left teaching at each step, wisdom and love.

'Each life and each being of this universe has a great mission, to give Love and to be happy; with every little smile, with all hope or wish of peace towards what surrounds you; you fulfil a part of that mission, the mission to give and to receive Love, and you have done it, you are doing it in this moment and you will always do it, because it is your essence. It does not matter where you are or how you do it, because for Love there is no time or space. It is an infinite energy that we all have in the Heart.'

The old lady answered with great excitement: 'Why do you say this, if all my life has been painful and bitterness? I never thought to do what you are saying now. I was so hurt by the rejection of people that passed by me, that I ended up thinking I should not exist and that my useless life would be better if I had not lived it; with this I summarise what I have been. But what you are telling me is so beautiful, it is like nothing I have ever heard before. You make me feel as though my life has a purpose, a goal, even though to me it does not seem clear. Something inside my chest makes me feel that you are telling me the truth and you give me much happiness, because now I know and feel that if my life ends here, I left something of myself. I do not know if it is good or bad, but it is something that, deep inside me, I tried to give when I did not even suspect it. Whoever you are, thank you for giving me these last moments of happiness. I know that something very high sent you so that I could say goodbye to this world, and to be thankful for the life given me.

'To know that there are persons like you, with so much Love...now I know that I did not live, I did not want to live, confining myself in my own world, losing the beautiful things of what is around me. But it has been worthy to have lived just for having you like this, at my side, showing me with your Love that life should be lived with happiness, feeling beautiful as you told me, beautiful just by living and feeling. Thank you again, and you can be sure that, wherever I go, I will always remember you, my Angel…'

The conversation ended because, in that moment, the ambulance that would take the old lady arrived. They put her into a small bed and the Master was beside her until the ambulance left. In his eyes there was a kind of sadness, but also great happiness, knowing that part of his Love was able to go in different ways to her and make her understand her own beauty and the one that was around her.

The next day I talked with this Master, who I call Blue (it is not his name, but it is the colour of his energy), and I asked him about this old lady's health.

'She left this world with much happiness and with a little sadness,' he answered, 'but that helped her to find her new course and to continue her great way…'

He looked to the sky and his eyes reflected a certain nostalgia and happiness. I asked him what we humans could do to give so much love and tenderness without prejudice, as they do. He answered me with a sweet smile: 'All of you, the children of this Earth, have infinite Love in their hearts, Love that most of the time you try to hide because it could mean weakness or simply through fear of being rejected. It is very important that each being discovers that beautiful part which, for generations, they have been taught to hide, and through time has been hidden under the ignorance. You have been made to live ignoring this infinite capacity of Love without limits, of a universal love that lives in your wisdom and in your hearts.

'The beautiful old lady lived most of her life in great suffering, ignoring completely the reality of Love that lived inside her; she despised herself for not having being loved, at least not in the way she thought. She felt hurt and rejected by others. However, her inner being, which she would not listen to, told her about the great commitment she had with her own being, with others and with this Earth. That made her subconsciously wish to help and give others what she demanded for herself.

'One day,' Blue continued, 'she had struggled to get a little bit of food at a small helping place in order to get food she had to be there long hours under the rain and cold weather. Finally she went towards her shelter to eat without being disturbed, when on her way she found a blind old lady who, like her, lived on the streets from the charity of others. She was sitting out in the cold weather and when she passed by her, she told her: "Why are you here, if it is raining? Come, I will take you to that roof." With much tenderness she took her to a secure place. When she did this the blind old lady asked her: "Are you one of those persons that help poor people and feed them? Is that the reason why I can smell food? Is it for me?" The beautiful old lady put aside her bitterness and with great conviction gave her the food. When she did this she felt a great peace and happiness, and it was too much even to consider it as a reality, so she decided to forget her and to regret what had happened and of her weakness.

'However, she never forgot the help she gave to that old blind lady and, each time sadness came to her, she immediately remembered that rainy afternoon when she was weak, but happy. That action accompanied her up to the end of her life, and it filled her with satisfaction. And she would meet again with that old blind lady, to whom she had called yesterday, as angel face...'

When the Master said this, I felt my body shiver and my throat closed; as soon as I could I asked him: 'Does this means that the old blind lady was you? I mean, did you disguise yourself as an old blind lady to prove her goodness or something like that?'

He answered me with a beautiful smile: 'Yes, I was the old blind lady, but I did not disguise myself, it was rather her who did it.

'Those moments were very difficult for her, because she was in a very difficult stage in life that would had caused her more suffering if she could had not been able to understand her reality, that forgotten reality, her goodness, her wisdom and her ability to give love, all which she needed to keep on living; so she asked herself to live this condition, to prove that she was still capable of feeling something for others and to love. She asked me for help and I gave it in this way, and the love she delivered me was so much. When giving me her food and when she kept me protected me from the rain, she opened – without knowing – a way of always being with her up to her end on this Earth that she loved so much...'

After I heard the Master's words, I could not talk. I thought about it and I tried to understand better each phrase he told me, to comprehend in all its excellence, that great teaching and his actions. Still today, when time has passed by after that conversation, when I remember, it touches my Heart profoundly, and each time I do it, I know there is a new teaching to learn and assimilate.

There are many love attitudes that Masters have towards each living being on this planet. These attitudes are – without any doubt – great examples for everyone. These teachings inside each love action give us a clear idea of the great spiritual evolution of these beautiful beings. For them, evolution is just Happiness and Love. There are no steps, or ways to define themselves; however, their actions define their true and beautiful mission.

Many people ask constantly that, if there are angels or beings from another planet, why do they not manifest themselves to everyone? There are many answers, in fact there are many theories regarding this. However, for many others, their 'non manifestation' means they simply do not exist. We do not realise that they have always been here, and the ones that have always closed the only door to that relationship are us, the current 'humans', and not them. The communication between two persons is not only talking or standing one in front of the other; the true communication is the one that starts in the real conscience, which we still do not understand.

Our actions have become less conscious, our attitude is more mechanical and our vision more limited. If we add to this the fact that our Heart is considered of less importance, and has given its function to the brain (where it does not belong), we can conclude that the capacity of our being is completely reduced by our actual way of living.

The Masters try to approach us in different ways, with the necessary subtleness, so that the corresponding part of us can perceive them and make the connection from Heart to Heart, the only language of the universe. Without this way of communication and attitude, it would be impossible for us even to try to understand them. That is why they are asking us to return to what we are, to our source, to that divine essence, forgotten in a corner of our being because, when we do this, we will finally return to our reality.

Wisdom of the Heart

The sons of the volcano

Another experience of love and great teachings happened in Cholula, Mexico. We were in this small town near to the Popocatepetl volcano, because at that time it was showing some activity and the energy was very strong. For this reason the Masters were here permanently, to help in harmonising through electromagnetism, with the purpose of avoiding an eruption that would damage completely the entire planet.

They allowed me to get just to a certain distance from the volcano because the energy flows were too aggressive for the human body; but these conditions were easy to take by the Masters because of their great knowledge towards their own body and essence. The purpose of this approaching was to learn the great quantity of liberated energy and its effects on the beings of this Planet.

This meant a need for me to be near the Masters of great wisdom and love, who for hundreds of years had been living in the volcano, for the purpose of producing vibrations which help to liberate the great and immense energy it emanates. To know that Masters had been there for a long time was a big surprise for me, but most of all to see how their presence was accepted by the villagers, most of them indigenous natives of this place.

I was sitting on the grass trying to apply the Masters' teachings regarding energy and sensibility. I tried to see and feel what was in this entire place, not without asking first our nature brothers' permission. The Masters were some yards away making a kind of prayer towards all nature in this place and to the Great Volcano.

Suddenly I was very startled upon hearing strange voices, which did not emanate from the Masters, and I immediately looked to see from where they came. I could

see then, that two old men and three indigenous women
natives from this village were speaking with the Masters
with great happiness reflected in their faces, and I noticed
a great familiarity towards them. This really amazed me,
because it is not common to consciously communicate
with the Masters, due to the quantity of unbalanced
conditions that we humans possess; this fact surprised me
and made me very happy.

I decided to get near them and, when I did it,
immediately the two men and the three women looked to
me with smiles on their faces. But what I noticed most
was their expression of innocence and love that at that
moment made me feel a very strong emotion in my chest.
I drew near them and saluted them, then they invited me
to sit on the grass, which I immediately did just like the
Masters.

The oldest man started talking saying: 'You are
welcome by the sons of this land, as are our Brothers
Goyitos (pointing to the Masters). You are surprised that
we are here, aren't you? (They all started to laugh.) You
should not be, because we have been invited by them, as
they have been by us, and that has been for ever since the
eagle and the serpent, the sun and the moon were born...'

Then one of the women explained: 'We have never
lost the communion with the heavens and the stars. Much
has disappeared, most of all the reality of our past and its
people; but we have hope that our brothers will give us
back that which has gone: respect and love that lived
amongst all the inhabitants of Mother Earth, and so to be
again one being, without limits...'

At that moment I felt great sadness for what they were
saying, because I had believed that it was impossible they
could express themselves like that. I felt bad for myself
because of my prejudice, learned from a blind society, as

is the human society. Thousands of feelings and thoughts passed through my mind; I did not know what to say.

It was then that the youngest of the indigenous women, with a beautiful voice, said: 'Do not feel sadness or pain for having a different appreciation of what we are. You know very little of what is the essence and origin of the land where you were born; the little you have learned has not been the whole truth. The wisdom of our ancestors has been buried, the same way a man who was assassinated because of his great power. But today, that great man has been helped to wake up and, by doing this, heaven and earth will at last be united, as they were before…'

After hearing these words full of truth, I felt a kind of vibration that went all through my body. I asked them: 'Have all the indigenous and native people of each community not lost communication with the Masters?' The oldest man answered me: 'Many of us have lost our capacity of listening to our gods in our hearts, of listening to the tzentzontle language, the singing of the river water, and all of this has brought us the blindness and deafness of our gods' things, and therefore the inability of living with our brothers from heaven. Not knowing the part in us of what we are, has made us also forget who they are, but the ones we still know - thanks to our parents and grandparents – we guide the other persons to keep or wake up to this reality, but never show this to the ones that still do not want to understand it.'

With these words, full of sincerity and kindness, I did not know what to say. Then one of the Masters said: 'Thanks to them we can be here, because they are the ones who opened the doors from their land, from their beings and most of all from their hearts, and made possible the mission of guiding, at least a little, the energy of this beautiful place. For the people of the big cities, the indigenous, the town people, live in a supposed "ignorance" that they have never even tried to understand. This has made them at the same time live away from society, a society that for centuries has judged them in a very unfair way.

'They have,' he continued, 'given much in all the aspects of human life, even if it is difficult to understand their contributions. The truth is that they have tried hard to keep the mother culture, the origin of each being, trying not to lose what still remains from their true essence. Their value and strength are worthy of admiration, even though they are seen with distrust by their brothers of this planet. They are always fighting to keep their traditions and their ancestors' wisdom present in their people for always.'

When the Master said this, I noticed that there were tears in the eyes of the oldest indigenous man. When he noticed I was watching him, he said: 'Our Goyitos, sons of the stars, have confirmed our path and mission in this life. They give us hope and love; they teach us with their presence that they are always with us and, as our churches teach us, every human being has an angel and they are those angels.'

I was surprised by his words, most of all because he referred to them as 'Angels', and I immediately remembered the story of the lady from Europe who, when she was helped by a Master, was able to recognise the importance of her life, and that she called him 'my Angel'. This made me think about the great mission that Masters, for thousands and thousands of years, have been developing on this planet, and who for most of the time have been identified as Angels or just as Light Beings, but without physical body.

Wisdom of the Heart

Even though these beautiful indigenous people were really attached to Catholic teachings, this did not stop them believing in the Masters, because their hearts did not believe in limits that had been taught to the societies of the big cities.

This was a great experience of love and relationship, which taught me that the only ones that do not know, or do not want to identify, the truth of what is around us, are the ones that believe they identify the ignorant, when there is no more ignorant than the ones that fight to hide and ignore reality, even with evidences.

The Masters' presence and company in our planet is a reality that all of us should take into consideration, because it goes beyond our religious beliefs or philosophic concepts. Their presence is evident in each aspect of our life; each one of us has lived a moment or encounter with someone that left 'something' that maybe we will never be able to forget. A smile or some words might have relieved us or given hope, without even suspecting that it was someone so special, as they are: beings of great love and wisdom, that the only thing they ask and what they fight for is our happiness.

Unconditional love

I remember with great affection one of the love stories of the Masters, which happened in a small town in Mexico. We were in a very magical place, trying to learn a little about the beauty of this place full of wonderful things, that nature had created with all the wisdom that it is capable of.

It was then that one of the Masters, who have been living here for a long time, told me: 'Every afternoon comes a lady that is our friend and for a long time has helped us in everything with her happiness, love and sweetness; and lastly she brings us food, water, clothing and anything else she can give. She does this with love and humbleness, without expecting to receive anything more than our well-being. I would like you to talk to her.' I immediately accepted, because I knew it would be a beautiful experience and a great teaching.

When the lady arrived I noticed she was an old person. She was around eighty years old and she looked very humble, with old and patched clothing, but very clean. I immediately felt a great tenderness for her; she walked in a very fast way, although she had a smile that showed great peace.

We were a total of four - two Masters, one female Master and me. When she came she greeted us with her sweet voice: 'Good afternoon, I am bringing your corn flour drink, nice and hot, because the cold weather is strong, but for sure this will warm you up. Now I can see that someone has come to visit; if I had known, I would have brought you some little bread buns, but tomorrow I can bring you some...'

The Master immediately approached her and took the cup. Thanking her, he smiled and said: 'Thank you for all your love and for thinking so much of us; as always your actions are full of happiness and love, an attitude that helps us continue with this work, and thank you forever. She is Flora, our friend, and she is also helping us as you are, so you will see her around here very frequently...'

The old lady answered: 'I am so happy that you are here. You do not have anything to thank me for, and it is a pleasure to get to know you, nice lady...' When she said this, there were tears falling from the eyes of the woman. She looked profoundly touched by the presence of the Masters and by knowing that she was helping.

Wisdom of the Heart

She turned to me and continued: 'When I was a little girl I used to come to this place to play and to gather what I could find to eat and take it to my parents. I suffered to think that maybe I would not be able to gather anything, because we were really poor and were always hungry. At that time I entrusted to our 'Virgin Mother' so that she could enlighten me and I could find something to eat; sometimes I returned with nothing, but almost all the time I could find something to eat. When I looked at the trees, the birds, the sky, I could feel that there someone else than them by my side; I felt that my body shivered because something was telling me that there was someone there, although I could not see anything. So I did this for years.

'Later I grew up and got married. My children and I always came here, because I was hoping to be able to see or maybe to feel what I always knew was in here. Time went by and with the years and many worries I forgot about this place, because I could only think about my problems.

'Then, one day, when my husband had died and my children were living their own lives, I felt alone and sad; I fell asleep and dreamt that I was in a place like paradise. I saw birds full of colours, horses the colours of the rainbow and then I realised there was this beautiful man, with a long white robe, with some other people like him; they appeared to me smiling and told me: 'A beautiful and special place is waiting for you, feel happy and let your heart smile again, we will be waiting for you'.

Suddenly I woke up and I cried like a child. I did not understand my dream. I thought that maybe I would also die and I hoped that this could happen, but suddenly it came to my remembrance the place where I used to go for food, and which for a long time I had not visited.

Flora Rocha

'Then, I came through this way with a great emotion, wishing to find consolation; when I arrived at the place where I used to sit and look for food when I was a child, I ran into Them (pointing to the Masters). I saw them and I did not know what to do. I felt that my dream was becoming true and I gave thanks to the 'Holy Virgin' and to God, because after so many years I could understand what I had felt since I was a little girl.

'I know they have strong reasons to be here,' she continued. 'I do not know them, but I feel them and I also feel that they have come from far away, and that they have always been here, because I always felt them and my grandmother too; and as we need help, they also need it. How can I repay the happiness of feeling like a child again, with the hope to see, know and most of all feel that I had company, one that comes directly from the gods? That is why, as long as I live, I will help them whenever I can; they will always have a piece of bread and my heart…I have talked too much, right? But I do not speak about this to anyone because they would call me crazy. I know that you understand me, and I will always be thankful for knowing this before I go…'

After telling her story I, as always, did not know what to say. I was really touched by her words, her experience and encounter with the Masters of this place. I smiled at her, trying to say something, when she then told me: 'Do not worry, do not worry about saying anything. They have tried to tell me things, but I learned that words do not exist and are not necessary when the heart already has the answers; I have learned this from life and from them. I would rather not have the answers, but have a happy heart happy…'

When she said this, I was even more surprised by her words and her way of thinking; I then understood the great and infinite love that we as humans, and all the beings from the universe, feel, but for different reasons or circumstances we prefer to hide and limit.

The words and attitudes of this beautiful lady taught me much; just as the Master said, I learned from her humbleness and unconditional love, wishing with all of my being that this remembrance would always be in my heart. Up to this moment, this beautiful woman is still helping (within her own possibilities) the Masters, to fulfil their mission of Love and help, giving what is most beautiful: the Heart.

Chapter 4

Reincarnation

Through all of these years there have been conversations or situations that have taught me much of what we have been doing wrong. Much has been written about reincarnation and karma, subjects that have always been with us and which ancient writings make reference about.

Because of my ignorance on this subject, I thought that reincarnation was the process of rebirthing in human, animal or plant form. This concerned me, but I did not pay much attention to it. It was not until the encounter and relationship with the Masters that I could understand, comprehend and feel the importance of knowing this.

At the beginning, it was hard for me to understand this because it looked simpler than I thought. I believed that talking with Masters about reincarnation would be complicated, because they had shown me texts about it and it had been a little bit hard for me to understand them; even though the definitions were the same in essence, they were interpreted in a different way.

This is why I want to write about reincarnation (even briefly, as this subject would fill a whole book because of its importance), as for many people they believe it is true, while for others it is only fiction.

For a long time, reincarnation has been understood to be the rebirthing of the soul, although for some people it represents their resurrection. Most of all, in East, reincarnation has a much higher value than in western cultures, where we have suffered the loss and destruction of codes and sacred writings. However, we did not forget entirely this truth from our spirit. Our own wisdom – in many cases – has tried to remind us of this reality as a fundamental part for the development of our life.

All of us, at least once, have had that beautiful sensation of past-lived episodes, of faces that we have never seen before that come into our thoughts, of words and memories of something that urge us to remember. This, like many other situations in our life, is totally unnoticed and, without knowing, we let go of the opportunity to listen to our own past that can tell us the mission of our life. This is a reality, a reality that has been with us, but human beings have only been limited to believe in death.

One of the things that has surprised me is the fact that everything is connected with the mission that we beings have. It is not only for the children of this Earth, because this is a law in a universal level; it is part of the First Universal Law for all the inhabitants of this infinite Cosmos. This Law is the Law of Happiness or the Law of Love.

When we are born we have this great mission in our spirit, because it is part of this commitment for life and creation. This mission is simpler than what we think, because this mission is simply to be happy. Happiness is the purpose and the reason of life, but we humans have complicated it by thinking that happiness is just something that can never be, a fantasy worthy only of children and naive people. This has made us believe that happiness does not exist and that it is just a mental state.

We are born on this planet by our own decision, with the mission that has been appointed since the moment of our creation, the one of being absolutely and completely happy. This infinite and wonderful happiness should be fulfilled and lived in all its intensity in the life in which we are born, because it is our universal commitment. Our mission as infinite beings is to live in our essence, and that essence is Love and Happiness.

For many people – and this is the way it has been handed down for centuries - the reason for life is evolution. Evolution and evolutional beings have been referred to as something that we all have to reach and ascend to, what some call Glory, Heaven or Nirvana. It is something that in a way has made us believe that it is a special kind of preparation of a spiritual 'work' that will take us to that evolution. This, without any doubt, has been fundamental for many when deciding to move away from a path that is supposed to be difficult and complicated; most of the people think that you should become a kind of monk or to dedicate yourself to meditate day and night to reach this desired evolution.

With the Masters, I could see and understand that all human beings are born with a great energy; this very pure and evolutional energy – if you can call it like that - is our wisdom. She is always in our heart, our spirit and essence, something that we lose without noticing, until we completely forget that it is inside of each one of us.

This complicates the fulfilment of our mission with the planet and universe. We draw further away from the happiness of our life as we continue separating from ourselves, from our essence, and from all that is around us which, at the same time, is a fundamental part of our life and our mission.

Evolution, in simple words, could be defined as the capability of being happy and giving others this happiness. If I wanted to define Masters, it would be as completely evolutional beings, because they possess the capability of enjoying and loving each thing, small or big, visible or invisible. Their great will of loving and being happy for that infinite love is what makes them seem, to us, as the most evolutionary of beings.

Sometimes – at the beginning of our encounters - I asked Master Nintancito how they all reached those levels of evolution, to which he answered me: 'The evolution you talk about, for us is just being happy. The great energy that flows from each one when enjoying and loving what surrounds you, is an energy of infinite proportions that opens many doors and ways inside you, so then you feel that you are the Infinite, that you are created and creator. This feeling is what transforms your own way and all that is beside you, making you vibrate inside, of the mission that all we universal beings share: To Be and to make others happy.' This helped me understand something of that Evolution that, for Masters, means happiness.

We can now understand that happiness is a commitment, being the reason and mission for our existence. When you come to the end of your life and you discover that the motive and reason for our being here on Earth has been forgotten, and that maybe the desired happiness passed us by and we let it go, it is then that we understand that we still have an obligation and debt with our own existence. But maybe the time in this life ended because we have death as a law on this planet.

We will have to come back to this Earth, to try to fulfil our mission of life, to be happy with all our being and spirit. If our mission was not fulfilled, we will be called again by this Earth's laws as many times as is necessary so that we can fulfil that mission and discover that, if we are here, it is for a great reason, and that reason is to be happy and to make others happy.

Some time ago in Spain, when I was speaking about this subject in a conference and mentioning that the main mission of man is to be happy, a person felt offended by it and said to me: 'How can you assure that happiness is the reason for life, when the reason for the universal beings is evolution, and the ascension of dimensional levels? You cannot say that the only reason for living is JUST being happy.'

When this lady said this, somehow I understood why she was so upset and I tried to explain it by asking her a question: 'I agree with you in what you are saying, but what is evolution for you?' She was a little surprised by this, and she answered: 'Evolution is ascending, to let go of our needs and our traumatic events in life, to become evolutional beings to ascend to superior levels.'

I said: 'I agree with you, but for you what is the purpose of this evolution?' She answered saying: 'To liberate ourselves, to ascend.' So I asked her again: 'Yes, I understand and agree, but then why is this evolution? What do you mean with this evolution?' She answered, a little bit angry: 'To get to Unity, to enjoy getting to ascension.' To that I answered: 'I agree, but is that not called happiness? When you reach those levels, to evolve is nothing more than the capability of enjoying and loving what we are and what we have, that is the reason for life. Therefore, that is our mission, to be happy and to make others happy. We should not make things more complicated, which we have been doing for so long. The evolution in a being is measured by the capability of giving and feeling love, there is no evolution than the answer to this love and that answer is Happiness.'

Happiness can mean different things, however. I heard from Master Nintancito a meaning with the essence of what really is: 'Happiness is the feeling transformed in emotion and action, which fills he who calls and provokes it and is also capable of sharing it with all that is around.' Then, I understood that happiness is what does not affect others negatively; on the contrary, it is capable of contributing to the happiness of those around us. Unfortunately we know little about this, because we think that our joy comes before others, and by doing this we are moving away from our own happiness.

This is the reason why communication with our most sensible and wise part is just as important; that is our heart, because he is the only one capable of guiding us to love and to do the correct things in order to reach our full evolution in happiness. We should not deny and move away from something that is the reality of our being. We all, in any kind of way, are involved in this search; we all desire love, the well-being of our family and our environment, even though we believe in resentment and hate, but inside each one of us there is this pure feeling of love for EVERYTHING. Some of us have separated more than others, but that bit of light is still there.

We must remember that our family is not only the one we think we know, our family is all, what surrounds us, what lives inside and outside of each one, inside and outside this planet; so in the same way, let us love what is asking to be loved, because that which is asking for love is ALL that inhabits this universe.

How beautiful it is to know that to fulfil the commitment that we have, as children of Mother Earth, we only need to be happy and to love. We only need to allow ourselves to be who we really are, to remember that our creation is infinite and immense, and that what we have wanted to see of our life and of our Earth has only been a minimum part and may not be the real one.

Wisdom of the Heart

So our work and search is just beginning and it should start with our heart. Our voyage on this planet should be the opportunity of living and enjoying this life, fulfilling the essential mission of our being. Happiness is infinite and eternal, therefore this mission is endless, it goes beyond what is beyond, and in each step we, as universal beings, fulfil our essence, our mission as creation and creator, the one of being infinitely happy.

This obligation as universal beings is that which makes us return to the place where we could not fulfil that essence and mission. If we are still here it is because we have not completed our mission on this planet. But we are alive and we have the rest of our lives to end our mission and pay with happiness and love our stay on this Mother Earth.

Karma

The subject of karma is also very important for our life. Surely most of you will have an idea of its meaning; however, there is a lot of confusion about this. Through centuries it has been spoken about as 'the Law of cause and effect'; that rules everybody's life; for many it is a reality, while others who are more sceptical see it as a way to scare us, with the idea of causing evil. However, this is one of the real laws that is part of the human essence and rules our life in a determinant way.

Karma has often been linked to reincarnation. In interpretations of sacred ancient writings - particularly Oriental ones – it is clearly mentioned the connection between our past actions and present life. For thousands of years it has been believed that if someone was born with a physical imperfection, or suffers from poverty, hunger or pain, then karmic law is responsible for that disability and is capable of giving an answer. The answer is that a painful life is for the payment of karma and probably as a result of a past life. When having a physical imperfection it has been believed that in a past life that person probably harmed someone in the same way, and therefore it is making this person pay for his or her 'mistake'.

This might seem, to some point, connected, or is the only explanation for pain and suffering. Maybe it is because of this that many societies and people look upon this law as a consolation, feeling that they cannot fight against 'Divine will'. For ages we have believed that suffering is a way of purging our punishments and learning, and that this will make us think that to 'deserve' being happy we must first pass tests of suffering. Many people accept suffering and pain and offer it to the Creator to achieve forgiveness and to reach Him.

This false belief has spread to enable the human being to be in control of dark forces, and has taken away from us our universal capability of Wisdom and Strength.

With the Masters, I realised how wrong we humans are on this Earth. They have tried to teach us and guide us to our wisdom, which would show us that the most important things in our lives have been misinterpreted.

Masters know that 'the Law of cause and effect' is real and that it rules at a Universal level. Unfortunately, we are always fighting between good and wrong, terms that are found in religious and philosophical concepts. Therefore, if Karma Law is a universal concept, we could say that thinking, feeling and acting have a clear interference in our life, above all in human beings, because we are capable of having the most confused and opposed feelings, thoughts and actions.

For the Masters, this law logically will never apply,

because their actions are always based on Love and Compassion, and their path is lit by their Infinite Love and Wisdom. They live to fulfil their mission as universal beings, which is the same mission as ours; the only difference is that they are aware of it and therefore they live at the full extent and with the infinite love of their being.

For them, karma is a law of commitment that rules the lives of people, because this connects with the energy law, if I can call it that. Each movement, thought, feeling and action causes an energy that connected by our actions and all that we are. All good and wrong that we do in our lives will definitely have a reaction that will reach us, with the purpose of making us feel where we are going, and above all to be conscious of whether we are fulfilling our mission to be happy and to make others happy.

As we know, our actions determine our present and future, and what will come into our life in a short or long term will depend on it. But the belief that our current shortcomings, or the cause of a human physical deformation, are the results of karma is a misinterpretation that has lasted for centuries.

The Masters explained to me that karma, as we understand it, has been deviated from the real way it affects us. It is believed that a person has been dragging karma from life to life; it is like a merciless collector that will follow us with our debts beyond our death and new rebirth. For the Masters, this is one of the bad interpretations that have harmed us through centuries. If a person that intensely believes in the karma law, interpreted in this way, is born into poverty and a suffering environment, by believing that these conditions are part of his destiny and karma will make this person agree to suffer and pay, denying himself the most important mission of his being. This person will be wrapped in a cycle of lives not lived, at least not within his mission of happiness.

Karma is a law of cause and effect; there is no doubt about it. It is something that rules us and can only be applied in the present life, not in the past, because the opportunity of rebirthing will give us another identity, and it is for the purpose of fulfilling our mission of being happy. If we had to carry karma from life to life, without any conscience of what we were and did, we would be paying for something that we do not know and have ignored. At the moment of death and being born again, our spirit is the same, but the conditions for the physical life will be different, with circumstances that will make us understand and feel what our mission in this life is.

Throughout life we manage to pay, through the law of cause and effect, all that we should pay before dying; our essence and personality of what we are in this life are responsible for our actions. The moment we die and leave the physical body, we also leave all what was negative that prevented us from being happy; it is then that we are in the pure and whole conscience of our real being and of whom we really are, returning to our essence and pure life full of light, Wisdom and Love.

During this stage, we start reviewing what we were and did in the life we just left. In this moment, the person does not need someone to show him his mistakes, because when he is in the real essence he will be able to recognise all that we did not do with Love. Each thought and attitude away from Love and happiness produces a great pain and sadness in the one that is in the process of reviewing his life. This feeling turns into a great force that makes this person realise that the mission as a universal being was not fulfilled. Then he understands that he will have to come back to his planet and serve with his part of Love.

His birth is a new opportunity to show the real being, the wisdom and infinite Love. He could not come to this new life with the debts that, in this instant, do not exist anymore; at the moment of encountering the real being, he had the opportunity of recognising his mistakes. This is the reason why he will be allowed to live again on the planet where he did not fulfil his mission.

His karma will stay in the person who he was and was totally paid in that past life; so the law of cause and effect will start to rule again in his new life.

Only in the case of those who have committed murder, the law of karma works in another way. Cutting the life of another person is one of the worst things that can happen, and in these circumstances the price to be paid is very high. Usually, a murderer will never have the conscience of knowing the great damage that he has caused, because his subconsciousness and a complete distance from his heart and love had to be the reason for doing something like this. These persons have closed all the ways of light to them. Maybe society's laws will make them pay for what they have done, and obviously the law of cause and effect will collect the price for the crimes. But this price is nothing compared to what they will live and feel in the moment of their death.

When he separates from the body, mind and personality, in what was his material part, he will remain only in his real and pure essence and will be totally incapable of feeling something which is not the love of our creation. It was separating from this which caused him to commit a crime; facing his reality as a universal being and to that infinite love from his heart will make him confront the most profound pain and sadness when recognising the harm done.

At this stage of meeting again with his real essence, all the images of love and hate will be shown to him and, in the case of a murder, he will feel the pain of the person that he killed and, at the same time, the pain of all the persons that were affected by this act.

There are those who might think that this is not enough for a person who commits this kind of atrocity. We are sometimes capable of recognising our mistakes, but it is difficult for us to take conscience at every level of the damage that has been caused. However, when we leave this body loaded with what is not part of our creation and we meet with our true being, our feelings are immense and infinite as our love, and therefore we have the capability to feel, live and regret the mistakes as well.

It is a process of infinite pain, because the person that takes a life is an assassin in what was his life on Earth, but not in spirit and essence. It is like if a being full of light and love has a kind of dream and, when waking up, would realise that he committed one of the worst acts, and yet felt himself completely incapable of doing something so low. However, he knows that it was something that happened due to the subconsciousness of recognising his true essence and denying love.

Therefore, this person that has transformed into this kind of being will be for a long time in this suffering, until he assimilates his crime, his pain - that is, the pain of his victim and his family – and has transformed into light, receiving the forgiveness of his victim.

Then he will have to pay his debt of Love that was not paid during his life, and will come back to it with a new opportunity to repair his crime with Love and light. His karma will begin with his new life, in which his spirit and essence will be more committed than ever to fulfil his mission of Love.

But it is here where karma takes different forms, because if this person relapses in deplorable acts of hate or moves away from love like murder, his past karma will join his new life. This happens because he himself has merged his last way with the new one to make from them just one. With this he makes his past crime a misdemeanour in his present life. Then he would have to pay a debt that had already been paid in other levels, but now it will be under the law of Cause and Effect. In this way, his own life will make him compensate in a terrible way for his lack of conscience for forgetting again his true mission of Love.

Only in this kind of situation is karma carried from life to life, but most of the time this is limited only to the life we are living in. However, making the same mistakes is a common thing amongst human beings; therefore it is totally necessary to be conscious of our existence, knowing the wonderful mission we all have.

As I said before, trying to give answers to pain and suffering has been, in some way, what made us take the law of karma as an explanation. However, karma does not go from life to life; I can now say that the reasons for so much pain, sickness, violent and unjust deaths, etc., are due to the huge imbalance which our planet has been in for thousands of years.

The Masters talk about illnesses (as science explains it) as the result of different imbalances that have been affecting all the inhabitants of this Earth. All that which is negative or capable of causing pain or sadness was born due to this kind of negative energy, as a result of the imbalance. Unfortunately, we human beings are the only ones responsible of most of these low energies.

The imbalance of the planet, which is affecting every

aspect of our lives, is found all around us and, like in a game of chance, can fall to any of us. Of course there are many influencing factors for this to happen, but if a baby is born blind, it is not his karma that is punishing him, rather it is the disequilibria of this planet that has ruled his life since his conception. That is why there are more misfortunate births now, because the imbalance of this Earth is growing bigger.

Violent deaths and all that which can cause suffering are not a divine will, and even less the will of a higher being. All the things that are inside the limits of darkness and pain are situations created by us. Therefore we are the only ones responsible and capable of destroying those imbalances. In this lies the importance of taking responsibility for whom we really are, to fight with all our strength to recover what we once were.

For many people there is no such thing as a 'god' or 'Supreme Being'. They feel that if such a being existed then there would be no injustices or pain in the world. This idea is very unjust, because we should remember that one of the main laws of men and universe is free will. We, as divine creations, have the liberty to decide our path; our actions are not judged by anyone, only by ourselves. However, this Supreme Being, or Universal Creator, is so infinite that it helps us and that assistance has always been with us, but we have always preferred to ignore it. The magnificence of nature in all its many forms is part of this help we get from this Supreme Being, but it seems that we do everything possible in order not to acknowledge the reality that it can show us.

Now is the moment for us to discover this reality that is infinitely wonderful. It is now the moment for us to open the door of our heart to ourselves to enter an infinite universe, full of love and wisdom. We should remember that laws have been created by the beings from the universe as a way of aiding the unity of the Infinite.

It is important also to consider the help and guidance of these beautiful Masters and ask our hearts the reason for things. We should try to forget the ancient interpretations of subjects so much transcended, such as karma and reincarnation, because the most important thing is and will be, to fulfil our mission: TO BE HAPPY AND TO MAKE OTHERS HAPPY. We should always strive for this, because this is the reason for life.

Whatever our religion or beliefs, we should always remember that the reason for life is not suffering, and it is not through this that we will be able to ascend. The only things that will enable us to reach the most infinite places will be Love and Happiness. It is not relevant to know who we were in our past life, the important thing is to feel and remember that we are here again to finally fulfil our mission. It is necessary to remember that our essence is infinite and that never dies.

We should not forget our mother root; we should not forget why we are here, or the mission of our creation. This will assure us that we can change with our love the world's imbalances and, in this way, we can destroy the pain and suffering that we human beings have. It is in us to return the absolute beauty and the light to this Mother Earth. Paying with Love the life that has been given to us will make our world what we have not allowed it to be, only full of joy, Happiness and Love.

We can achieve this, because within us a great strength lives that, up to now, we have not used. Our being is screaming for this, to free the truth that exists inside each one of us, to obtain in this way the happiness that would be for ALL and, in union with the universe, continue our path towards the Infinite.

Chapter 5

Who are the Angels?

A very important part of this book is that we may learn more about these Masters, whom I have talked about since the beginning. Their presence here on Earth –as I said before - has been documented by past civilizations, even though all that we know about Them has not been considered or has been taken as a myth, taking away any value.

We have always heard about Angels and their presence in our lives, from the moment of our birth to our death. For many, they are a part of reality, for others it is just a religious belief. However, their existence in our lives is a reality, reality that most of us do not remember, and has been ignored by our subconsciousness. Much has been said about them, making them non-reachable beings for us, because most people consider them as ethereal beings or composed of only energy, not matter.

To understand a little about this I would have to explain that, for us, matter is what we can perceive by our senses, or the opposite to the spirit. If something is not perceivable we take it as non-material; if, on the other hand, we consider that it is spiritual, we immediately unbound it from matter. This has caused us to believe that angels have no body or any kind of matter like ours, thus we 'make them' into non-reachable beings thus setting a big barrier in between.

Flora Rocha

Everything that exists in the universe is energy and it is also matter; it may not be like what we know, but it is still matter. The nature of it will depend on its birthplace; unfortunately, our planet is one of the densest places, because our way of life and thoughts define very important aspects of it.

Our bodies and all that surrounds us are matters of relative density, while our thoughts are more negative or destructive. Thus, our matter becomes harder and rigid, and the opposite happens with those persons that live a calm, peaceful and happy life, inside and outside of their being.

Much has been said about our astral body, which can be defined by many as ethereal matter. This astral body is our true 'vehicle' – if we can call it like that – but this vehicle, as opposed to what it is believed, is a body made of a much more subtle matter than the physical body, and the real essence of our being can be found in it.

It is the inner part, but it is not intangible, as it is believed. It is our most subtle matter and creational body that has been given to us as the reality of whom we truly are. We need to have a great strength of Love to achieve in our physical body what we are in our astral or spiritual body, but unfortunately we live divided.

Our astral body is part of this universal essence; it is our connection with the Infinite and all its creation. Although opposite to what is believed, it is not only when we are in sleeping states that we can be in the astral body. We have divided our bodies, believing they are incompatible; when one takes action, the other cannot, and this situation is far from reality.

We are simply a same being, with presence and matter from the place where we were born, and also with real presence in the universe. It is true that when our physical body rests, the astral part (this is really the part of wisdom and strength) has the opportunity to travel to its roots that unites it with the universe.

If we human beings could break a little with what has been established by laws and thoughts that we have inherited generation from generation, we could discover the wonder of what we are and all that is around us.

There are true and serious records of the omnipresence of persons that had been seen in faraway places from where their physical body was located. To achieve this, we need a great communication with our Heart. Unfortunately, for the current inhabitants of this planet to achieve this is almost impossible, although there are some people that can do this because they are living inside their own wisdom and in harmony with themselves and their environment. It is possible for them to communicate and live with other people as if they were in a physical body, because their astral body becomes material, but subtler, in that can be touched and seen by others.

Our ancestors lived in perfect harmony with themselves and their environment; therefore they had this conscious manifestation of their astral body. Much has been said about certain plants and how they could help our ancestors to achieve travel with their universal being. But it was something more than help that they asked for: they asked for guidance from the essence of Mother Earth and its protection to go out in their universal body. They never entered into states of hallucination; on the contrary, they were reencountering their own being, where neither limits nor restrictions exist.

Once I was in a very special region in an Indian territory with a Master, who was a spiritual guide of great wisdom. When talking about this subject, I remember that he said: 'When we sons of Mother Earth were born, we had to wear its welcoming outfit, which is this beautiful body. It has strength to confront its pain with great resistance, intelligence to know how to take advantage of what it gives us, and it possesses a great heart which is our connection with 'The Infinite' and the source of what we are.

'This physical body that we see is the representation of the four laws and forces of this Mother Earth, and it is necessary to be able to live in harmony with them. That is why it is given to us when we arrive here, and when we inhabit it we conform to the fifth force, which is the force of 'The Infinite' and the Universal Creation. We should not forget that this body is necessary to fulfil our mission here and, in order to accomplish this, we need to love and live with that being we really are inside this outfit, since it is ourselves in universal creation.

'We acknowledge this commitment by what we are inside and outside. Our grandparents have taught us how to live with our earthling environment, as with the universal one. We use the guidance of our Brothers of Nature to do this, since they protect our journey in our beautiful being; without them we would not get that protection and that light to go through the paths of the universe. This way, we will never forget the reason for our presence here, our mission and loving the environment as we love ourselves.'

With this, I understood that we human beings have forgotten universal principles of true importance. We have a presence in the universe, not only in this body or for what we are, but because this essence and original creation has been with us always. We have never been separated from this original condition of our creation. What is deplorable is that we have forgotten that it is part of ourselves.

So, then, why is it so important to know and acknowledge that our astral presence is more than just an untouchable energy? Why should we recognise that our divine essence can be seen and touched in any part of the universe? What is the connection of all this with the angels?

To begin answering these questions I should say that it is very important to acknowledge that we are not just a body, a spirit or energy; we are all of these together, but we are also beings with infinite capabilities which we have tried to ignore. There are no limits of any kind, just those in which we have chosen to believe in. We should begin to live with this forgotten part of what we are, because it is fundamental to find by ourselves the wonders of our creation. This way, we will discover that we are a same being, with a body that believes in limitations and another with infinite possibilities of manifestation and creation.

Those dreams in which we have wonderful sensations of flying or encounters with unknown people, that leave in us a great emotion, are not just something that is produced by our mind; they are not just something that our brain liberates. Instead, they are signals that try to call us into this reality, our universal reality. Unfortunately, all these signals are weakened by the little importance with which we regard them, thus forgetting about them.

If we achieve more consciousness in what we are inside and that part of us that is not often considered, it is then that we will have the opportunity to acknowledge and understand our angels. Our ignorance of this subtle, but material, body we possess does not let us understand or simply believe that angels are non-matter beings that, therefore, cannot be seen nor touched.

The angels, as they have been called for millennia, are beings of great wisdom and love, who have always been with us and have tried to be our friends and counsellors. These angels have a physical body and they also have in their lives the mission to be Happy and to make others Happy, and because of this they dedicate their lives to accomplishing it. Their physical manifestation, even though it is subtler than ours, is the same body that we human beings possess. Therefore, to notice their presence is not hard to do if we are connected with our own subtle essence; however, the images that we have created of them have made it more difficult for us to recognise them.

Many centuries ago, the presence of these beautiful beings was part of daily human life; however, since we turned them into a myth and the news spread of their 'celestial and magical powers', it was decided to give them a different image, due to human being's loss, little by little, of its universal reality and his connection with the Infinite. When we were in the process of forgetting our capability of acknowledging and acting with our essence and wisdom, transformed into the magic that we now call fantasy, we were also withdrawing ourselves from what still was magic. When taking different paths, we decided to lose touch with reality and we were immersed in the supposed 'truth' that prevails up to now.

Without doubt, this was the beginning of our subconscious reality of what we are and what is around us. Our angels went from being our friends and guides as a reality, to be mythological and untouchable beings. The ones that believe in angels believe that communication with them is difficult or that maybe they will never get to see them or touch them, when it is not like this; on the contrary, our angels are looking for ways of making their presence noticeable for us.

Maybe what is most important is not being able to see them in physical form or to be able to touch them, but to know they are absolutely real beings, and that they live and feel the same way we do; that their presence is so evident as it is what surrounds us, and that the more we believe they are unreachable beings, the more barriers we are placing between ourselves and our understanding and connection with the wonders of the Infinite and the universe.

I think it is necessary to meditate upon this, because the divisions and limitations of our being have taken us to lose communication - at least on the conscious level – with beings of Great Love and Wisdom, who have been at our side always. With this, we lose something that is part of our being, and that is to bond with life from the universe.

Our angels, far from having wings as they have been represented, are beings that fight to take us towards our liberty, to remember and feel that limits do not exist, fear does not exist, that hatred does not exist, but only Love, that First Universal Law, a reality that we have wanted to forget. Our angels guide us, just like a big brother or our best friend would do, unnoticed by us. They are our Masters that try to guide us towards something that is already inside, and that is our Wisdom of the Heart.

This is why, when I have the great joy to see the Masters and to be with them, I know they have been our Guardian Angels that never abandon us and that they will keep on fighting for that day when we will all be capable to waking up to reality, the reality that is in front of us disguised as a Fantasy. This is the reason why we should break with our own limitations, to jump over the walls that do not let us see beyond, and reject anything that separates us from our universal brothers.

The mission of our angels is very extensive and I believe that not even in ten books could I capture even a portion of that great work that they do for our benefit. But the most important thing will be to take the first step, discover that their presence is real and tangible; that our angels can be at our side and that they can go by completely unnoticeable, as our angel, friend and protector.

Their wings and all that we identify as part of the angels is more the representation of the liberty that they want to give us, to raise our being and to finally be able to acknowledge our beautiful origin. This allows us to throw away all the weight from this body, to separate the burden from it that has made us so dense, and therefore enjoy our universal essence. Above all, to enjoy the wonder of living with beings of complete Love that dedicate their lives to our wellness, fighting to take us to our mission of Love and happiness, and with this they fulfil their beautiful Mission. Let us open the doors of our being, let the barriers fall and with all of our being let us embrace our beloved Master Angels.

Chapter 6

These are our Masters

After seventeen years of living and having experienced for the first time the approach and encounter with the Masters, I can say that their presence is something of high importance for us, the sons of this Mother Earth. Their work - as I have mentioned before - has been diminished, tergiversated and ignored. Their mission is very clear: to help us find our own essence and wisdom, and by this recover our path of Love and Happiness.

Very few of us humans are set to find a solution to our problems and, least of all to give them Love. We have forgotten the basic principles of respect toward ourselves and our environment; with this behaviour we have done much harm throughout the history of our planet, and the sad thing is that we still continue with this attitude. Thus, it is not strange that beings of Great Love and Wisdom, that can see and feel our pain and confusion, want to help us.

Any one of us that loves their brother with all their heart would be able to give and sacrifice their own life for his brother's sake, only caring for the possibility of helping the loved one to find the path of light. And so, this is what they have been doing for so long; their mission towards us is almost unknown and for many it could just be fantasy, far away from the supposed 'reality' in which we have been taught to live.

However, it is not logical to still deny something so clear as the reality of our Masters, when the only thing we have to do is to look back to our ancestors' records, and take away words like mythology, beliefs, fantasy and superstition. These concepts have been set to tergiversate a truth that has been kept dormant for thousands and thousands of years, hidden under preconceived definitions by our eagerness to disregard all that we do not understand. This has taken us far away, not only from this magical and wonderful reality, but from ourselves as well, to the point of not knowing who we are at all.

If we start by acknowledging and opening this part of our being, if we start by opening ourselves to the reality of beings of Great Love and Wisdom, we will then be opening a part of us that we have not known about and for sure this will marvel us. At the same time, this will make us feel free, infinite, with the capability of seeing, hearing and feeling the wonder of what is around us and of our magical creation.

With this small book I hope that all I have learned these past years can be transmitted to each one, not letting any dogma nor belief interfere, as this does not interfere with any; on the contrary, it is the essence of each religious practice or philosophical thought.

The Master's teachings, their guidance and their Love are for everyone, and we all have the right to know that there are beings that love us in a very profound way; that their only purpose is to guide us with their light towards our own light. For them, the work they are doing is no sacrifice, it is just happiness; their dedication towards us is infinite, that is why I have titled this book's chapter 'These are our Masters...', as I will show you a small part (because their mission and work is very extensive) of the beautiful work they have been doing for thousands of years.

To be able to write about each one of the Masters that I will show next, I had to be with them most of the time all through these years, learning from them each step, each action and, above all, trying to know how to capture something so wonderful, that most of the time is so difficult to describe.

Undoubtedly the words of a wonderful Master as Nintancito have helped me: 'Be happy, live in your essence, your heart is your guide, infinite force of your being; if your heart writes, then you will only write words of wisdom that will go from your heart, to the hearts of those that feel and live in the reality of their own being... Thus, they will live each word and that feeling will show them what is most important, their own wisdom...'

These beautiful words have been my guidance and strength all the time that I have dedicated myself to write, placing first – more than good grammar – my heart, the love and admiration that these beautiful Masters inspire in me. So, I hope that this can be taken as what it is: a beautiful reality that cannot be ignored anymore, a reality that will give us faith and hope in our future.

Lady Master Dcim, the Master of children

This beautiful Lady Master is accomplishing her mission in different places on our planet. Her main purpose is to help the children of our Earth. She is in charge – with many more Masters – of taking hope, light and love to each little child. However, her work is centred on any little girl or boy that is going through any pain or sadness.

Her mission is limited by the lack of ways in which she can manifest her love, because unfortunately we

Flora Rocha

human beings have closed, with strong barriers, the ways of communicating with these Masters. For many, her work and the work of other Masters would be like the so-called Guardian Angels, which most of the time have been seen or felt by children, having with this the opportunity of becoming great friends and helping them to keep going through a path of hope and happiness.

Maestra Dcim.

90

Wisdom of the Heart

The time that I was with her was wonderful and full of great examples of knowledge and strength; this is because of the incredible dedication they have towards our little girls and boys. Masters consider the childhood stage as fundamental for the development of the human race; unfortunately, this is one of the stages in which we start to teach children a world that is totally different than the real one. Adults try to show them their 'reality' and, as a result, move far away from their own essence.

That is why the Master's mission consists in showing to our children, in a subtle way, that fundamental part of their being and of all that is around them. This of course will depend on the conditions that circumscribe a child, because most of the time it is we adult people who are the ones who close the doors toward these Masters.

The mission of the Masters, who dedicate their life and work to be near the boys and girls, is so necessary, even though it is hard to explain such admirable work. Unfortunately, most of us adult people direct the path of our children through the same path as ourselves, which most of the time is full of mistakes and which, for sure, our little ones will continue and imitate.

Children have a great need to know and learn about what is around them, and most of the times we, the adult people, are not prepared to teach this and to give this guidance. Masters then try, through daily life and in their astral body, to talk and live with them, hoping they can keep that part of light, strength and wisdom of their being, and that in the future they will be capable of guiding themselves with their own wisdom.

Many of us – maybe in our memories – have seen an unknown face that at that moment was important, because it gave us a smile full of support and love. How many of our children or even ourselves have lived a magical moment? It is something that is hard for us to explain and that, because of this, we have tried to forget; how much magic in our lives have we let go because we have not been able to explain it, without knowing that we are shunning something so important and yet it has a great reason for being in our lives.

Much has been said about these 'invisible' friends - at least, that is what they are for adult people – that appear to children by helping them, playing with them, and talking about things that maybe we adults do not talk about anymore. For many parents this has been a worrying matter, because the 'invisible friend' of their children is something which is impossible to believe and to handle properly.

The first reaction to this is fear, that maybe the child has an emotional trauma or maybe that there is a negative entity (this should never be laid aside, however, as the child's attitude will indicate us what it is). In this manner, parents act in different ways to correct it, such as using psychological therapy, by which children learn that what they do is wrong. The little ones feel obligated to hide it or maybe they learn to fear this situation and close any relationship with these friendly Masters.

Lady Master Dcim is a woman with so much peace and love that it is very hard for me to be able to talk about her; her love and dedication to our children is endless, this is as well as with the thousands and thousands of Masters around our planet that are performing this same mission for our little ones. Their work is tireless because the suffering that millions of children go through on our planet is too much, from lack of love, understanding, food, home and so many more needs that we all know.

However, the presence of these Masters has made a

difference that for us is hard to see. Their love labour is something that we should never forget; on the contrary, we ourselves should join in this because even though there are many people on this planet who are doing this same mission, it is still not enough.

First of all, we should be aware that it is not only intellectual education and food that is the most important, but also guiding and giving Love; we should take children to their own nature, so that we can take them away from the limits in which we adults believe. This is a fundamental part and unfortunately a forgotten part by most of us. This is the reason why our lovely Masters try to fulfil their mission and try to fix this mistake, but most of the time these opportunities are restrained by us.

I was once in a beautiful place where this Lady Master is at the present time, to guide the support that is given to children. I had the opportunity to ask for her permission to write about her in this book, to which she immediately consented with much love. Therefore, I had the opportunity to live with her and to understand her mission in a more profound way and to discover the endless dedication they have for children.

I know it is difficult to express in a few pages a mission so infinite and great as the one the Masters have. However, I hope that this is just the sparkle that opens the heart of each one to understand what cannot be written here, but that undoubtedly it is in our hearts.

I remember that Lady Master Dcim told me about the great importance of being near our children and, along with them, to approach our own essence. She told me that the pain that many of our children have to suffer on this planet is too much. From sicknesses, wars, mistreatments, abuse to even losing their lives at the hands of adults who, in their own childhood, were also abused and guided through the way of hatred.

She expressed to me that in order to end so much pain that our children are suffering, we adults should try to change, as we are in charge of their guidance.

I remember with much sadness a story that this Lady Master told me. She told me with sadness: 'It is necessary that you, the sons of this great Mother Earth, open the eyes of your hearts towards all the terrible injustices done against loving beings, such as children; they have suffered much throughout the years because of the blindness of those who should be their loving guides. There are so many callings for help and much need of love by them that we would want to do more than what we can. However, there are so many insuperable limits and barriers, set by the adult people, that many times we cannot ignore them, making us very sad for not taking action, as we would like to. Your children's necessities are not impossible to cover; on the contrary, it is much easier than you can imagine, the only thing you need to do is to love them and learn to laugh with them.

'A nine-year-old boy, due to the lack of love from his parents ever since he was born, lived through violent moments. He had a big communication problem with all those was around him. When he was alone, he talked to his clothes, to his bed, his hands - he needed to feel that someone loved him, and that this love was not destruction. His parents talked about the great Love they had for each other, when the only thing that he witnessed and heard were yelling and violence, which many times was directed at him.

'Sadness flooded his heart more and more each time, and because of his lack of communication he was considered to be autistic. This caused the situation at home to become even worse; his parents intensified their violence, believing that the boy lived in another world or that he did not understand what was happening.

'The little boy suffered terribly. He asked for help, help from anything that was around him, and because of this I was able to reach to him one night. This was after a great amount of work, because his life was surrounded by hatred barriers put there by his parents and, above all, because of the lack of faith in something magical and infinite. I was finally able to reach him, and this did not surprise him, because he in a way knew someone would answer his call.

'I got near him and embraced him in my heart, giving him strength and love. He started to cry, holding me with fear and desperation, saying: "I knew you would come, I do not know who you are, but I know you can help me. I do not want to be here anymore, I am afraid, take me to the place where I was before I was born. Please do it. I just needed a smile and a hug full of love from my parents, I just asked for them to love me as I love them, but they do not care, that is the reason I want to go away from this world, it is ugly, it scares me. Help me!"

'These were the words that the little boy said, but in that moment his father came into the room with great angriness and hate in his eyes because he heard his son crying. He did not notice my presence, he was so blind in the presence of his confused emotions that he neither could feel me nor see me; the little boy told him with great fear that an angel had come to rescue him and that he was going away, but that he would always love him and his mother as well. His father felt great pain, which he transformed into more hatred and confusion, wishing with all his strength for any presence that he did not understand, that it would not be real and that it could disappear.

'His heart tried to tell him how wrong his attitude was, but he did not want anything more than what he knew, which was confusion and rejection towards everything. With this, he made my presence with them to be impossible, because he was closing the only way that I had found to be able to reach the little one. Then, I went away, but before I did so, I gave his son part of my strength and the endless love of the universe so that he could illuminate his life and take his strength, and I asked him to fight against his pain. Afterwards I gave this energy to his father as well, wishing it could make him reach into his light.

'When I left, a part of me stayed there, the pain of this boy was so big and the action that I could take was so little, that for the first time I felt what you, the sons of this Earth, call sadness. We do not know these feelings, but when entering your world, under your laws, we have had to live painful situations and learn, even inside of this, to change them for Love and happiness, because this is the only way of true help for all the inhabitants of this beautiful world.'

When Lady Master Dcim finished telling me this, I could see sadness in her eyes. This situation really moved me. I asked her what had happened with the little boy, and she answered: 'His heart and mine are connected, as it is with all the beings of this Earth, and our communication still continues, even though for him it is difficult to be aware of it due to the fear that exists in his life.

'The physical and conscious approach to him, as with so many other children, is difficult because the ways that lead us to them are full of obstacles for us. But when their fears rest when children sleep, our connection is intensified and we try to give them happiness and love, to achieve a liberation of their fears that can help their bodies rest from so much pain and can continue with their lives, even under adverse circumstances.

'Our presence before them is, most of the time, through encounters in which they ignore who we are, but we get to be a lady that with much love gives them candy and a smile, a man or a girl that with some words can relieve their pain, or the hand that is ready to help when there is a fall. We do this labour of Love with our infinite essence, but this labour is very limited, because it is something that only you can do with great success. Your children are suffering; they are walking to nowhere, ignorant of the true reality of their being and presence on this planet, which takes them to a confusion that will harm them.

'It is necessary that you direct the lives on this Earth, to face all that is asking you; only you, the creators of the destiny of the lives of each boy and girl that inhabits this planet, are the ones who can take their lives towards their true path. Our presence here can only help to show you what you still do not want to see, and in some events go a bit beyond and be able to delay the blindness effects: but we cannot change your way, the path that waits; only you can decide to walk through it.

'Our mission is to place the signals that indicate where it is, but to follow them can only be your decision; because of this our presence is now more evident, and it just wants to show you that there is much to discover, and that within this discovery your future of happiness stands, the Happiness of this Great Mother Earth and its Sons.'

The words of this Lady Master showed me that it is now time to take control of our lives and take up our responsibilities as universal beings. The help of the Masters is everywhere, even inside the most unthinkable situations; however, their mission of Love for our children is worthy of our recognition, and this can only be through the Heart of each one of us.

All of us that live on this planet, without doubt have received part of this unconditional Love from these beautiful Masters. Our childhood is full of magical experiences, some painful, but I can assure that the Masters' Light and Love has illuminated our paths and up till now they still do, only hoping to give us that Hope and Faith, so that we can give those qualities to each child, starting with our own.

I also remember these beautiful words that Lady Master Dcim shared with me: 'All that you have to do is to think of your sons and of the children of the world, and this thought will fill each one with your Love actions; and so, each action done will be a gift of Love that will help transform your world into the world that each child dreams about. Then that hope will stop being just a beautiful dream, but will transform itself into a beautiful reality.'

If, some day, someone gave us a beautiful smile, somebody comforted us in our weeping, or if that unknown person told us 'you are capable of reaching the moon', then we can be sure that Lady Master Dcim and other Masters have been and will always be with us.

Master Lazmew, Master of Art

One of the most sublime aspects of the essence and sensibility of our inner being is, without doubt, the manifestation of art. The different ways of artistic expression are a clear and real reflect of our own being, of those feelings and thoughts that live in our essence. Because of this, to the Masters, art is the manifestation,

Wisdom of the Heart

universal communication and expression of our spirit that takes us to paths that we do not know about, streams which are full of our origin.

Maestro Lazmew.

Flora Rocha

The representations of Love, Compassion and Happiness have their most clear expression and manifestation within the art that has been developed on this planet. Since the beginning of time, the human being has expressed his feelings and thoughts through this universal language, capturing it through drawing, painting, sculpture, singing, dancing and other endless ways of expression that helps the human being communicate something beyond the limits of language.

Art is a way of approaching our universe, as well as to the external and internal infinite; maybe because of this, within these expressions, we can find the support and presence of many Masters. One of them, who is in charge of commanding the support and guidance of these expressions, is Master Lazmew. He is a wonderful dancer, in all dancing genres, although his main dedication goes to what we know as ballet. His mission specialises in helping anyone that asks for help in any place of the planet, all of this made through the way of artistic expressions, even though most of the time his presence is not considered or his mission is ignored. Like him, there are thousands and thousands of Masters that are doing this same work.

The mission of Master Lazmew is centred in taking this motivation to the places that are far removed from the expressions of art, because Masters consider them as a great therapy of togetherness with the heart, with all that inhabit this world, and of course with the universe.

To me, art has had a very important role in different aspects of my life, above all to understand myself more and understand in a better way the reality of this world and the universe. When I first met the Masters there was much fear in me, as well as doubt, confusion and many other emotions that we as humans experience. However, I did not know that all of this lived inside of me. Because of this (now I understand why), one of the first Masters that I knew and that I had the opportunity to live with, in those times of confusion and questioning, was Master Lazmew, the Master of Art (as I call him).

I remember that I had many questions and thoughts going through my mind, but the only thing this beautiful Master did was to ask me to draw what I was feeling in that moment, or to sing what my heart was singing. This really surprised me, because I was looking for answers, and so, no matter how much I asked questions or tried to evade doing what he told me, he would just tell me: 'Do it, do not be afraid, draw, sing, write, dance, do whatever you feel, but do something, because it is there where you will find the answers you are looking for.' Whenever he said this, I did not understand how I could find within myself that which I did not even slightly know. Through time and his great example, I understood a little bit more and knew that he was right; thanks to his guidance, I discovered that the only way to get rid of all that we are afraid to recognise, is through transmutation which art represents.

On these journeys with this beautiful Master, I learned things that were immensely beautiful. All were related with this infinite love that Masters feel for us humans, as well as their great patience towards our stubbornness and blindness.

He lived in Baja California, Mexico, until the energy of this place was appropriate for this. Now he just lives where anyone is in need of guidance from fears, joy, frustration and happiness through the infinite manifestation of art.

The art of 'Dance' is just one of the many examples of how art can do wonders for people, as well as for the environment. This is why I significantly remember a reunion with Master Lazmew in Asia, where dances within indigenous tribes have a very important role for protection and energy management, as it occurs also in the indigenous communities of America. At this event, I had the opportunity of being present at a dance that was very much like ballet because of the similar movements, and that really amazed me because it did not seem that the people from this community would have the opportunity to receive teachings on this art expression and be able to develop it in that way.

I asked Master Lazmew how this was possible, and if he had something to do with it, to which he answered: 'The different dancing manifestations, or what you call ballet, are universal manifestations of Love. In each part of the universe we can appreciate a dance taking place. Planets and the universe are a continuous dance, as our bodies are too, where each particle performs a majestic dance. We can all express our feelings through it, giving ourselves something magnificent. Not only the one performing it will be filled with love, but also it will flood within each thing that is around it. After that, it will travel with a great strength everywhere and it will go into each heart. Because of this, it is not necessary for them (the dancers) to take lessons of what is part of their own being; the only thing they do is show love and respect for themselves and all that is around them...'

I then understood what Master Lazmew was trying to explain to me, which helped me admire the beauty of that manifestation. On that trip I learned very important things that I know are hard to express, because they are so full of wisdom and love that written words are too limited. However, this entire book is an attempt of the heart to get across an idea of the magic that is around us and which we have ignored, or have not taken seriously.

I also remember words full of truth from this Master, in which he would make reference to what art should represent to us human beings but which we have ignored. It is important to recognise that now a more serious relationship exists regarding its importance, because the scientific community has set itself the task of discovering the benefits that art gives to the human being.

This is something that our ancestors knew and handled perfectly, to the point that there are magnificent creations that are impossible to reproduce by the human being nowadays. With this, we can clearly appreciate that current society has lost its direction; it has disconnected its own being from reality, to become lost in a world as confused and unreal as this.

Nevertheless, we have hope in recovering that wisdom which is hidden and forgotten within ourselves; there is still a chance to finally awake to the light of our world. We have many things that could help us do this, and one of those things is art.

It has been said that only a few of us have any artistic talent, and we believe it. However, with the Masters I have been able to understand that art is the 'Infinite Expression of Everything'. There cannot be a definition of art because it is totally infinite. It is in our creation, in our blood, in our own being. Our life is the most magnificent artistic expression; therefore, each part of us is a representation of Art.

Through time this reality has vanished, and now it is just in the hands of those that have an artistic need so strong that it impels them to dedicate their life to developing it, while most other people forget that it is a very important part of our being. With the simple fact of recognising and giving value as a way of art representation, to our footsteps or to the way we move our hands, we will be opening a great number of possibilities and, above all, of wonders that we have ignored about ourselves.

We humans define art as the ability to create something or simply as a system of aesthetic norms; however, it is much more than that. Master Lazmew explained to me that art forms in our planet are limited and only considered for intellectuals, when really it is far from being this way.

In his own words, he expressed: 'The true essence of art has been lost between definitions and expressions that many times are far removed from its reality. What you call Art is the manifestation, expression and materialisation of Love, it is the sublime and direct way to give this powerful energy to all that exists, to the 'All Mighty Infinite'. The Love manifested and given through an artistic expression is the greatest help for Mother Earth and all of her sons. Remember that the manifestation of art is appreciated and cherished by the human species, because it represents the connection and communication with nature, with Earth; they will always be thankful and will cherish each gift that comes from you, their big brothers...

'Your Parents of the past knew this and lived in harmony with their universal being; their life was connected completely to manifest and capture in art, all their love and respect for what was around them. This took them to live each part of their existence on this Earth with all the happiness for being able to fulfil their mission as universal beings, knowing with each part of their feelings and of their own being. The biggest heritage that they have left us from this Wisdom of their hearts has been left in the traditions of their towns and its people, as well as in each construction, in each object that has all this energy of love and wisdom that speaks of their great dedication to happiness and to their universal origin. The mental and intellectual interpretations of heart expressions have caused its definition to be far from its reality. But the reality of Love is only the universal reality of Love, and with this there are no limits, as equally as there is neither guidance nor teaching that can take you to it, because it is something made by creation and will be a part of each being...'

Masters also talk about the importance that art has in all aspects of our life. The energy that moves and is generated, starting from the creation and manifestation of any artistic expression, is so big and infinite that it can move and transform many of the things that are found unbalanced around us and inside ourselves. As an example, the painting of an artist is something that, if it was done with true feeling, this same feeling will be transmitted to the person that admires it. Maybe the viewer cannot consciously capture this signal, but in his energy there is going to be a conjugation with the creator of the painting. He will receive a quiet teaching that possibly later will influence his life, as help or just as an alert to the experience lived by the painter.

The wonderful thing about art is that its expression is infinite and most of the time there are no barriers of time, matter, space or language. In any place that a dance, a body expression, a painting, a sculpture or any of the many art manifestations is appreciated, the message that is in it can be clearly captured.

Because of this, throughout all centuries, the Masters have tried to communicate through art part of this reality that has been forgotten and misunderstood. In this manner, the mission of these beautiful Masters of Art is infinite and will never end. The main reason is that for a long time it has represented the only way that we human beings have left open for that approach, not only with the Masters but also with this 'Infinite' that is waiting patiently for our awakening and, above all, for the happiness of seeing us happy.

We should not be afraid of manifesting our inner being through art. Let us break limits once and for all, and let us show to ourselves and to the 'Infinite Expression' that is around us, our beauty and our endless Love capability. We do not need long time sessions or long dedications to be great artists, because we already are great artists, we only need to acknowledge this need of expression, and manifest the magic that lives inside each one of us.

This inherent art that is asking us to be manifested has many of the answers we are looking for, because in its expression that magnificent and immense power part is present, the power to transform, heal, give happiness, Love.

I remember with great tenderness a story that I heard from Master Lazmew. He told of me of a person that was studying art and its influence. This person was German. He had studied, since he was young, art in all its expressions until he was considered an eminence in his field, which caused him to travel all over the world. But he was very much confused; he got to the stage where he could not understand, from his intellectual vision, the reason for art. He recognised that it was a necessity to express what cannot be expressed; however this did not satisfy him completely.

He was constantly travelling to Mexico and South America to meet with different ethnic groups in a search for their art as part of a research he was carrying out. This way, he was able to find different ways of art and expression so wonderful that he was even more confused. His search was part of something he could not understand; it was a great need for explaining art, even though he did not know why. He understood that art was part of something that cannot be explained, but his mind wanted more.

When he was visiting the Teotihuacan pyramids, as part of a research trip, something very beautiful happened. My husband and I were staying in a hotel very near this archaeological zone, in which this person was also staying. My presence in this place had something to do with my meeting Master Lazmew, because there are magical and wonderful principles of that region that I wished to learn more about in a profound way in order to better understand the expression of pre-Hispanic art.

I was in a meeting with Master Lazmew, near the pyramid named after the Sun. We were sitting, bonding with the energy of the place, when I noticed this German man looking at us constantly. I was surprised, because it was not often that the presence of the Masters could be seen by others; only on the very rare occasion would someone perceive something. They are simply not noticed, and people would not even suspect that they are Masters, which often helps their mission to be fulfilled in a better way. For this reason, when this man looked at us, I supposed that he knew something about Master Lazmew.

I remember that this man sat about three metres in front of us, looking insistently toward us. Master Lazmew looked at him with a big smile on his face, so I believed that the reason this man was there was because of something the Master knew.

We remained there, filling ourselves with the

wonderful energy from this place, when the man – who was looking at us in a more persistent way – stood up and directed himself towards us, which was why Master Lazmew told me: 'Open your heart, he is just looking for his path (he was making reference to this man) and his connection to the Infinite…' When I heard this, I knew that anything that happened could not only be by chance, but that it had to be this way for a very special purpose.

This man finally stood in front of us and, in almost perfect Spanish language, he greeted us and asked us where we were from. This surprised me and I answered that we were from Guadalajara, Mexico. Then, he immediately turned to the Master, waiting for his answer, while I, a little worried about what the Master was going to say, also waited for his answer.

Master Lazmew said: 'I am a neighbour of this Great Mother Earth.' The man seemed not to have understood this answer; however, this did not stop him from asking permission to be seated. Then, he gave us his personal data, his name and profession, and the reason for his trip. When he finished he said that he was waiting for us to do the same. As I did not know what to say, I decided to remain quiet and let the Master handle the situation, and something was telling me at this point that all this was part of something that had to occur for a special reason.

Within minutes, this man was relaxed and started a conversation in which he manifested his concern about the artistic expressions in the history of humanity. He said he was sure that there was a connection between science and art and that his purpose was to explain art through science. For this reason he had dedicated his life to this search, sacrificing his own existence.

While he was talking, Master Lazmew listened carefully to all that he was saying. This man talked about different things, very intimate things which I believe could only be said to himself, but the influence of the energy of love and understanding of the Master helped this man to talk about something that, for a long time, had remained very deep and in silence.

A couple of hours went by without us even noticing. If this man had not by chance looked at his watch, even more time would have passed. When he saw the time, he apologised and felt ashamed that maybe he had interrupted our activities, saying that he could go away if we had something else to do. Master Lazmew answered: 'Our presence in this magical place is just for one reason, and it is the one that we are living right now. Thank you for opening you heart, your most inner feelings and all of your immense being...

'I understand your search, this eternal search to connect something as subtle as the art of feeling with the physical laws of this Earth, but this connection you are trying to do through a scientific explanation or definition is something you will not be able to achieve. The reason why, is that science laws and the ones from the heart have never been divided; you have believed that it is like this, and because of this you believe that they are separate expressions. Science is for you the knowledge of all that is around you, its phenomena explained through laws that would show their principles and what caused them. However, because of how you defined science, you also limited it. The separation of feeling and the wisdom of your hearts have made you believe that science and emotion are separate forms, but it is not like that...'

I remember that this man was listening carefully to each word that was said by Master Lazmew. His expression was one of happiness and, at the same time, of confusion; he would only nod his head, as if he was begging for the Master to continue. Master Lazmew went on saying: 'This connection that you seek, of apparently separated forms, is something very important for you; it is a search in which you will discover that the laws of humanity and the laws of Love are just one. However, you must remember that your science is limited to what is infinite and that it should be able to break through those limits to be able to explain something immense.

'Something important for you to know is: what is art for you?' To that, the man answered with some doubt: 'I have asked myself this many times without reaching a definition. I know that it is something so big that any explanation would make me feel unsatisfied, but I know as well that our science has a logical answer to that expression and its reason why. It is this, the reason for my search of more than thirty-five years, that has made me feel lost.'

In his words there was so much pain that I felt he was about to cry, and he felt a little ashamed to have this manifestation of sadness or frustration. Then, Master Lazmew took his hands and said: 'You are a great man, who has fought to integrate that part of you that is asking for the connection of great forces as the laws of humanity and the laws of the universe. Art, as you call it, is the great manifestation of Love and all that this infinite force does in every being that is capable of receiving and manifesting it. It is a need of the soul, of the heart, of the being.

'Creation is the most splendid art, and that creation in this world as in the universe does not stop; it never ends, it is infinite. This is why everything and each part of your life is the most perfect art, and it can only be translated into happiness, which is the most beautiful art of the universal being.

Wisdom of the Heart

'These artistic manifestations should not be taken only as a part of human talent, as they are much more than this. Art itself is a part of creation and of the essence of life; its power and strength are infinite and capable of transforming any situation. It is the most beautiful gift that you can give to yourself, as well as to all that is around you; do not limit it to a simple definition, because its infinite meaning can only be understood by the Wisdom of the Heart and can only be lived through its infinite creation...'

As this man was listening to these words, he suddenly started to cry like a little boy, making the Master take him in his arms with such an immense Love, that it was extremely touching. I did not know what to do; I just let my heart marvel at such words from the Master and the Love that the sincere tears of this man had produced. I do not know how much time went by like this, but the image of all that was around us could not be more beautiful; the sun appeared to shine more and the pyramids looked as if they had acquired a special colour.

Without doubt, that experience and, above all, the words which were loaded with Love and Wisdom from the Master, helped this good man to be able to find his way in life, and made him fulfil his mission of taking art to all the countries in the world with all the magnificence that only Art can give. He would always keep in his heart this magical encounter with Master Lazmew, Master of Art.

This made me realise that there could not be a better art manifestation of the pre-Hispanic humans, than those great edifications created through wisdom, harmony and relationship of Love between humans and Nature. In that intense hug of Love and fraternity between the Master and this man, an extraordinary manifestation of love took strength through the pyramids, from the love and recognition of the infinite expression of art.

This edification was made only with the purpose of honouring the Universal Love, the relationship with the 'Infinite Expression', as well as to give a special and infinite tribute to the Great Mother Earth, Mother of all human beings. And so, is there a better definition of art, than that coming out of the heart of each one?

After this beautiful meeting, the German man could finally give permission to his heart to feel infinitely in harmony with his creation. And the most important thing, which was also said by him, was that he could discover that art is not limited to the expressions of Museums and Art Centres, because it is infinite and wonderful; rather it is also the art of living, the art of hearing your heart beat and, above all, to be able to manifest it and give it to others as the most infinite and beautiful gift there is.

But the artists of the past, as with the ones of the present, those who dedicate their lives to expressing this inherent art through the different forms of manifestation, without doubt have a great responsibility. It is an endless commitment with themselves and everything that is around them, because they are like guides, givers of Joy, teaching, wisdom, because art is one of the most direct ways of influencing society and everyone living on this planet.

Master Lazmew has explained and has shown to me that great influence. I have seen that this expression and creation, being part of that great energy of our being and so infinitely powerful, will definitely have an effect on the admirers or audience that open their senses to it. This was well known by many of our great creators from the past and they took it as a great responsibility, so they fought within themselves to generate and capture only manifestations that could mark guidance and knowledge for those that could feel their art.

As many know, energy is the 'Infinite Expression', therefore we are part of it, and we are also creators and generators of it. As I mentioned in past chapters, our actions, thoughts and feelings have a determinant effect on our lives and in everyone else that is around us and, therefore, also on our Earth.

Art, being a big part of this internal energy and strength of the spirit, will generate a huge power when manifesting through our movements, thoughts, painting, singing, dancing, sculpture and any other infinite manifestations. Then it will go to every being that is around this artistic creation, without matter, space or time being important; and this energy will be so powerful and endless that it will linger through time and have the power of transmitting infinitely the feeling of its creator.

In recent years, the scientific community has confirmed that art (especially music) provokes positive and determinant improvements to mental health, most of all in children. It has taken a long time for science to consider the great value of what cannot be touched, of what is produced through the heart of the people transformed into art. Mozart, as many other artists, has left us the heritage of Wisdom and Love through his wonderful emotion transformed into musical notes that comes from the wisest part of his being, his heart.

The power of music and art is infinite. With its correct handling through the awareness of its great power, it can help us infinitely in all aspects of our life. Because of this, the Masters have fought throughout time so that human beings can recognise its immense power and use it to help us find ourselves with our reality and to transform our environment. With this we will give a great gift to our planet.

We should not fear this reality. Let us open that part of our being that is asking to be liberated and cherished; it is time to recognise the wonders that are around us and also our own, beginning this way to generate more art in our lives, which will be translated into Wisdom and Happiness.

One of the things that the Master told me was that it is not only art that can be a manifestation of joy and happiness, as our life in this planet is in the duality, which is part of our creation as human beings. Sadness and pain are ways of expression that cannot be erased from our art, because art is the manifestation of the feelings of the human being. When we humans reach happiness, certainly our art will change and it will only be a manifestation of Joy, Love and Harmony.

Art is also a way of liberation. Through it, we can let go of our pain, resentment, anger or sadness. Then, that artistic manifestation will be in charge of transforming these painful emotions into a learning experience, and it would not have any intention of transmitting negative emotions. On the contrary, whoever receives it will be able to learn through this experience. This is what the artist feels in his heart, that his only purpose is to manifest what he feels, and not to harm through his artistic power.

It is here that the Masters consider that there is a great responsibility for all artists that dedicate themselves to showing their art to the world. Art is the most sublime expression of subtleness, and its practice should be guidance and light that should be of use to anyone that needs it. However, in recent times, art has been used to harm or to send a negative message, with which more confusion is provoked in those who admire its creator.

Wisdom of the Heart

This occurs especially among young people, who need a good example and guidance.

Our artists should feel inside of themselves the importance they have to the world. Many resist believing that they are an example. Since its conception, art is a determinant energy for everyone living on this planet, even if the intention is not to harm. The energy contained in this expression and manifestation will achieve its function, helping people or maybe confusing them more, depending on the case. I know this can be hard to believe for many people; however, it is something real and anyone can prove it if they open their hearts a little to feel all that we have denied to perceive.

Our art, which is part of each being in this universe, is one of the great benefits that we can give to ourselves and to our Earth. Throughout the centuries, the Masters have tried to remind us of its infinite importance, as well as its great power towards all aspects of our life. They have fought continuously, to the present time, with the only purpose of making us reach into that magical and powerful essence that we call art, so that in each song, in each dance or painting we can help others and help ourselves.

They want us to realise that we do not sing only to sing, that we do not dance only to dance, that we do not paint only to paint, that each movement and each word has an infinite meaning and value that will unite with the great energies of the Earth and the universe. This contributes to our creation capability of transformation of our life and our planet, with which we will enter in the frequency of infinite and wonderful Love, as it is our essence

So let us always remember when we appreciate a beautiful dance, sculpture, painting or literary work, to try to feel what its creator wants to give us; but above all we should feel that, in each part of art, the magical and infinite presence of the Universal Creator can be found, as well as the presence of Master Lazmew and of all the Masters of Art, which love us infinitely. They just want us to be able to recognise our wonderful essence and open our hearts to the 'Infinite Expression' and, with this, to unite ourselves with our universal essence without limits and barriers, as well as with all its creation...

Art can be this light that can guide us through the path of our mission: TO BE HAPPY AND TO MAKE OTHERS HAPPY.

I want to share something so beautiful and magical that I experienced whilst living with Master Lazmew. As I said before, he has as a way of expressing his Love through the art of dance, something very much alike to what we know as ballet. We were in a very gorgeous place, full of trees, near a very beautiful town. I remember that I had a headache but I tried not to pay attention to it, as I did not want to miss any detail of what was happening.

The Master then approached me and said: 'You know, it is time to dance...' and so he started an art dance. His body was something indescribable; his movements produced something that even now I am able to feel inside of me and it excites me profoundly. His face was completely illuminated with the great energy that was generated when doing each movement. He appeared to be experiencing great peace, but at the same time so much joy that it seemed as if this happiness he transmitted became something invisible that elevated him from the ground.

Also, his body produced movements that were emitted like shiny sparkles which travelled all over the site and beyond. A perfume was coming out of him, an incredibly beautiful essence. His hands were like a fountain that were generating and giving light.

Then, I clearly saw that very luminous multicoloured lights were coming out from his hands and towards me. I admired how these small and beautiful lights were passing through into my body, producing in me a shivering of some kind, something like a soft and comforting tickle.

As I felt this in my body, I experienced the greatest emotion, which filled me with something I do not know how to explain, something I could only call Happiness. The Master continued with his wonderful art dance, and was producing an immense quantity of light and harmony. All that was coming out of his body was in the form of light and penetrated everything in this place.

It was then that I could understand what I was not able to comprehend completely until that moment; the fact that people's energy is capable of transforming and filling with its light all that is around it when transmitting and expressing that Love. This helps to generate happiness, harmony and balance to all that is around it.

When Master Lazmew finished his art dance, he bowed in a sign of respect and Love to Mother Earth and to the environment, thanking them for letting him dance and give his Love. It was the typical salutation of dancers, only this was done with the true meaning that most of us ignore.

He came to where I was and asked me: 'Does your body feel better? Is your head liberated from its stress, and has your body permitted the entrance to the energy of the universe and of the Great Mother Earth?' To this I did not know what to say, as the excitement I felt inside would not let me speak. It was until then that I remembered my headache, which I did not notice had vanished.

The Master, knowing what I was feeling, just hugged me and I cried very much. I think I cried because we human beings have chosen to ignore what we are capable of manifesting and giving the most beautiful thing there is. I felt very sad because I was not able to know before about this beauty; however, I remembered the words of Nintancito when he said: 'It is still time to discover reality, it does not matter how much it has been unknown. What is important is to remember, and remember it with happiness...' With these thoughts my tears were transformed in an immense joy, a joy full of light given through the dance of the beautiful Master Lazmew.

Master Sabadimel, Guardian of Earth

On Earth, different energy centres of great power and importance exist for its balance and survival. These places, full of magic and energy received from the universe, have had a determinant role in the survival of our planet; thanks to them, Mother Earth has been able to resist so many aggressions from human beings. At this moment, more than seventy energy centres exist around the world, and generally they are located in areas far away from the big cities.

The area where Mexico City is located was one of these places full of powerful energy; that is why our ancestors settled their empire there, as they knew it was sacred land. Unfortunately, this area of strength lost completely its power since contemporary man has inhabited it. The big edifications, factories, pollution, etc., have been responsible for that strength to be extinguished and that only ruins remain of what was a great sacred place.

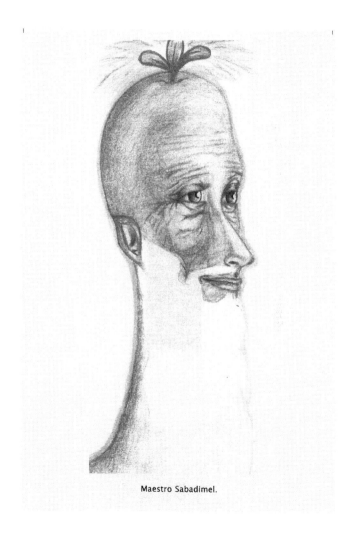

Maestro Sabadimel.

Flora Rocha

But these power centres of Earth are not enough to enable our Great Mother to heal her wounds. Just like in Mexico, the power centres lost strength, as happened to many other places that existed hundreds of years ago and, little by little, they have disappeared leaving destruction and unbalance in their place, without our Mother Earth being able to do anything to stop it.

However, help has come from our Masters who, with their technology based only in nature and their direct relationship with it, have been able to delay a little the devastating effects of our actions.

One of the Masters that is directly involved in this kind of help is Master Sabadimel. He is a wonderful Master, with Great Wisdom and an unconditional Love for all the inhabitants of this universe, but most of all for the inhabitants of this Earth. Living with him has been beautiful, full of admiration and Love, as in these seventeen years his patience and affection have been endless towards me; however what makes me admire him more is his sense of humour and his loyalty to his mission of Love. It is not easy to describe something that can only be defined by the heart and not with words, but I profoundly wish that at least a part of this can be felt through this book.

The reason I write about this Master is because his mission is and has been a determining factor on the life of all human beings. Maybe it is not easy to understand why, but if there is someone that could be called an angel or guardian of this Earth and its sons, without doubt it is Master Sabadimel. His mission consists in assuring that there always exists at least one way that can lead to Love, Faith and Hope for each being.

As you can understand, this mission is not easy if we assume that pain, the lack of Love and confusion prevail in most of humanity. But his battle – as the one of the thousands of Masters in all the Earth – has been a battle of Love against hate, happiness against sadness, and harmony against unbalance. The greatest obstacle that he has found is that we do not contribute to this battle of Love; on the contrary, we fight for more confusion.

But I would dare to say that the fact we are still alive today is because of the labour of Love that these Masters have achieved over the centuries on our planet. It has also been possible thanks to those few human beings who have dedicated their lives to do good to others; people that each day seem to be fewer in number, or perhaps it is that we need more help and guidance.

We cannot stop seeing reality. We cannot ignore so much pain that is around us. I know that there are people that only try to see the good side of life and that is wonderful, but we also need to realise what is happening, discover that the time of change has come and that there is no more time to think about it. This is something that has to be done right now.

This is why the presence of the Masters is more evident each time, with the hope that we can turn towards ourselves looking for that Wisdom. We are the only ones that can take us to the future, not to destruction, guiding us through the way of our mission, to be happy.

The energy we receive from the universe is so great and infinite, yet we have not tried to take advantage of it, even though this energy is capable of helping us find the way of truth.

As we know, our planet is just one of the infinite planets that exist within our universe, and its nearness to the other planets applies a determinant influence on them and vice versa, because the 'Infinite Expression' is interconnected like an endless chain. Many of these influences and radiations of great energy are of great importance for the planet, as the majority of these received radiations are large quantities of something that I can just define as Love.

It is nothing new that, for our ancestors, the universe – and its influence – was very important for their lives and their environment. Their relationship with these energy radiations was very important for these people; they preferred to build their cities towards that energy which, for them, was divine and sent by their brothers from the universe. This led them to build great reception centres of this sacred energy, with the purpose of distributing it all over Mother Earth, as well as to all its sons. The great pyramids and observation centres exist because of this, which were used with the certainty that only the wisdom of the heart can give.

This does not mean that in all these special places, edifications had been built; they did it only in places that were strictly necessary, because there were many more that should keep its natural state. But in many areas, what were not missing were the great rituals and parties which were carried out to welcome these energies. This had a great meaning for the people, because they knew their connection and communication with the infinite depended on those rituals and parties. I know this is a very scarce explanation for the great pyramids and rituals; however, my intention is to at least give an idea of what the mission of Master Sabadimel is all about and that it can be understood a little better.

After centuries of having this conscientious connection with the universe, there was a moment in which we lost it and never recognised the importance of the energy that is received from the universe. With this, we disconnected ourselves with all which was internal and external. Being connected neither to rituals nor to the natural way of life attached to the Earth and the universe, made us also forget that the power centres of the planet needed us and we abandoned them, thus harming our Earth in a terrible way. This is the reason why the Masters have been trying to keep alive these few places that still remain, with the intention that one day we will be able to take again what we left behind.

The fight of the Masters has been infinite. However, Master Sabadimel has said to me that the time for us to make our own way and recover what we have lost has come, because there is a limit to this help. These barriers have been set by humans, and they will limit the Masters in their ability to continue with their fight to preserve these places which are of so much importance for life here on Earth. If this happens before we take our responsibility seriously for keeping these places alive, the effect would be irreversible for all, including the planet.

I remember with affection an experience I lived through with Master Sabadimel in the Popocatepetl Volcano. This is one of the most important power centres of Earth, and also one of the most dangerous. Being at the volcano's feet, admiring its imposing beauty, suddenly the ground started to tremble. I began to feel scared, but I calmed down when I could see that Master Sabadimel had a smile on his face and an expression of admiration for the volcano when it discharged some steam.

The Master then explained to me: 'This beautiful volcano has been very important for the balance of Mother Earth. It is Her great wound healer; through him, she (making reference to Mother Earth) can let go of her pain and avoid falling into self-destruction. But in order for this to happen, her wounds should also receive the energy of the universe and this can only be done with your help, her sons…

'Through your energies, represented in dances of communication and connection with the infinite, is how Mother Earth can channel, through these wounds, the energy that you and the universe give her, and at the same time she can give you her energy of protection. Remembering and doing this again would be of great help for this Mother Earth, because the Love energy that she would receive from you would help her relieve her pain and, some day, finally heal what now is a great wound…'

He explained to me that volcanoes represent for Earth the releasing of her internal energy, as well as the channelling of the universal energy for the balance of life that lives in her. However, this has been completely forgotten and we have ignored our Mother Earth.

It is sad to say that, what for Earth were channels and centres of reception and emission of sacred energy, as time has passed by they have transformed now into big wounds that, in a constant way, are being opened and, through them, the pain and sickness of our Mother Earth are being liberated. Through time our planet has been in very painful situations and events that have provoked the communication channels with the inner part of the planet to close and, as a consequence, these ways of nourishment and energy liberation were blocked. This is what produces violent eruptions, when part of what the Earth receives is liberated, which provokes destruction and negative effects in the environment.

This is the reason why our Mother Earth is struggling hugely, together with the Masters, for those painful energy liberations to be stopped. But those wounds are dangerous and grow when the Earth activates and liberates its pain.

Wisdom of the Heart

This is where the Masters have been helping the planet and its inhabitants. Through great energy movements they provoke the relief of that pain through vapour liberations, which release great quantities of energy and avoid an eruption in the short term. Of course, they also help the ground where, through small sliding movements of the pressure mantles, they help to avoid serious earthquakes by liberating and provoking small adjustments that can avoid a big catastrophe.

The presence of the Masters in each of the volcanoes of the Earth is very important in controlling the effects which produce eruptions. However, their help is limited and many times they were not able to control some that have caused harm; this makes them sad but, at the same time, it gives them strength to keep fighting.

Master Sabadimel's mission is to help the ones that are or were great centres of power and communication with the universe. His main intention is to stop these energy reception centres of love and harmony from transforming into wounds or dangerous places for Earth and its inhabitants.

This help is hard to explain with words because it is so vast and beautiful; however, it is possible to define it as the giving of Love to all those places that have been forgotten by us, as well as helping to keep them active. The Masters do not stop fighting, even putting their own lives at risk, to keep the pain and suffering, that our subconscious actions provoke, from happening. It gives them great happiness to know that this fight can help someone to be happy.

Master Sabadimel and all the other Masters that dedicate their lives to this mission, work in a very intense way in each one of these seventy sacred places of this Earth, so that we can continue receiving the infinite energy from our universe. They consider that this is the way in which some day we will be able to remember the connection that has always existed and which will help us to create a better life for all that is around us and for ourselves. Because of this, their presence in power centres is indispensable as, through great rituals, they help to keep active each one of these places, from which our Earth can nourish and therefore survive.

It is not hard to infer that the knowledge and control of the energies and matter is necessary, not only the ones from this planet, but from the entire universe. With this, the right handling of balance and harmony is achieved, which for the Masters is part of their essence and life, but for us it is something that is kept forgotten in a corner of our being. Because of this, it is of vital importance to awaken all of our wisdom and to be able to take again our responsibility with life and Mother Earth, as unfortunately our planet knows limits through us, their creators, and her limit is close.

I remember that in one of these power centres located in Asia, I was with Master Sabadimel and five other Masters who lived there. They were trying to feel and recognise the force and energy that moved in this place. I have to say that everything is beautiful there, full of colour, harmony and, above all, Love; it is like arriving at an oasis that has not been touched by the human subconsciousness, a place full of the sublime force of the Infinite.

I could then see that near a place full of incredible vegetation, around twenty-one Masters with native people from this place were forming a circle. Plants were around them, and it looked as though they were also participating in what the Masters were doing.

Sabadimel said to me: 'From this place you are going

to be able to see the great energy of this beautiful ritual. Through each one that is inside of it, Earth will receive the energy that the infinite is sending, and at the same time she will return it to each one of them so that they can send it back to each corner and be a part of this Earth...'

Suddenly, everything was illuminated with very intense colours between blue and white, but soft at the same time, which reached into every part of this place making it look like something magical. It is hard to explain and understand. This great energy that illuminated everything was the radiation of strength that was being received from the universe; it came with all its purity to this spot where it was received and channelled by the place, by the Masters and by the native people.

When Earth received this great blue-white light, it was as if there was a fusion of matter with the infinite, it was something wonderful. Almost immediately, Mother Earth returned this energy transformed in a force that made my whole body shiver; it was so strong that I felt it was about to explode inside of me. I could see this force as a soft pink colour, so tender and with a wonderful scent.

The pink energy filled the place and, most of all, those which were participating in this ritual. The Masters then started to sing a thankful song with great love and respect to the energy that Earth was giving to her sons. Each of the Masters was full of this light, force or whatever you want to call it, which caused them to perform movements that looked like a harmonious dance that made the energy turn into a golden colour; it even looked as if real gold was coming out of their bodies.

This golden colour was of such intensity that suddenly I felt as if little gold leafs were falling everywhere. But the most spectacular thing was the sound of birds singing when a force started to come out of the Masters, which then transformed into all kinds of very beautiful birds and butterflies with intense colours that reflected us all.

This was something that I could never forget, because the birds and butterflies flew up to the sky and became lost in it, taking in their being its infinite and powerful creation for the sake of us, the sons of this Earth.

For a long time, I do not know how long, I kept trying to assimilate what I had just experienced. When I was finally able to speak, I asked Master Sabadimel what this ritual was for and what was created by it. He answered me with excitement: 'What you just saw was a welcoming and deliverance of the infinite energy ceremony, which in a constant way is received in each place that still keeps its strength, to channel it to each corner of this Earth to help life to exist... This energy will reach each one of you, wherever you are, even if you ignore it, because your heart needs it, for it is its connection with all that is sublime, which has been mostly forgotten.'

With these words I was able to understand how this energy comes, giving us strength and hope to fulfil our mission. The Master explained to me that this energy travels through the different existing vibrations and reaches each one of us, through our own power centres, which many people call Chakras. But for this energy to be able to come with all its strength and fulfil its mission of helping us to have clarity in our life, it is necessary for us to have an open and harmonious attitude. Where our receptive centres are blocked by our confused emotions and attitudes, the free access of this force will be closed almost completely.

I remember that Sabadimel told me that, when leaving this place to my hometown, I would find a clearer explanation regarding the action of this energy in people. With his words, I left next day knowing that surely something will help me understand everything better.

When my husband and I were at the airport, waiting for our flight that would take us home, a Spanish lady approached me. She first started talking about the weather and, after a while, we realised we were on the same flight. We started a pleasant conversation in which she told me that the reason for her trip was to relax and to get to know a little of the world, because her husband had died the year before and she was feeling alone. She told me that this country had helped her very much to understand and get over her pain.

I remember I told her she was a very brave woman to be able to travel alone to a far away country; she told me that she had never been like this before, as she was a person full of fears, although she knew she had to overcome this.

The conversation continued because the flight was delayed, and she told me, very excitedly, that the day before she had lived a beautiful experience in a dream. Her words were: 'Yesterday I did not know that today I would return home. I was in the village where I was lodged reading a book when, suddenly, I felt great peace that invaded me. I fell into a deep sleep and I saw myself in a place that I could not describe. I felt pain because of my husband, sadness but also happiness. I could not tell what was happening, but it did not trouble me. I was alone and I asked myself "What am I doing here? What good is life for me if I am not happy?" Then, to my surprise, it started raining golden leafs that covered everything, as well as my body. There were many beautiful birds that seemed to bring me a Love message that I could not be able to define, but that filled me with peace.

'At that moment I cried in my wonderful dream. I let myself be taken by this golden rain and what looked to be a dance by the majestic birds. The most beautiful thing was, when I took one of these leafs, when touching my body they merged with it. When I put it before my eyes it revealed all my life to me, but only the happy moments that I had lived since I was born. This leaf told me that my life continued, as there was much happiness waiting for me. I do not know if I have explained it to you very well, but it was like that. I do not know why, because I have never experienced anything like this. My happiness at that moment was huge, so much that I woke up with a sensation in my heart of hope in life and in me, which is why I decided not to travel the world but return to my country.'

When she finished talking, great happiness and excitement was reflected in her face from remembering this 'dream'. I was also very happy, because I had discovered what Master Sabadimel had told me about the ritual and the golden energy generated in it. I could then understand and feel more about how this great energy reaches us. Whatever the distance, it is helping us immensely to have the clarity and strength to discover our path and mission in this life.

My heart told me that this beautiful experience, so full of light, lived by this lady was only one of many that would happen all over our planet. The way that this Love manifestation by the Universe, Mother Earth and Masters can reach is infinite, and barriers that could stop the action of this energy do not exist. The only obstacles that can be found are the ones set by our own limitations and ignorance of the immensity of our being

The experience lived by this woman changed her life

completely and made her have strength and hope to be able to live a life full of happiness. Because of this, she does not let one day go without thanking life for letting her discover that she still had something to fulfil and had to fight for it.

Just like she was able to remember somehow and to bring to her awareness this experience, we can also achieve it; we only need to stop a little in our life and discover the wonder that lies in 'small' things. Many times it is not even necessary to remember; it would be enough for us to be carried away by these sensations of joy, or to have experimented something beautiful to help us live and feel complete and happy.

The energy of the universe received by Earth through these places and at the same time sent by Her to all of us, is also of vital importance for the places of great conflicts or where tragedies have happened. As we know, there are many places suffering from war, pain, hunger; places where a light of hope for those who live sad and painful situations is of vital importance.

For the Masters, these places are of such importance that sites of energy exist, where they are constantly in what could be defined as prayer. It is not the traditional prayer we commonly know – they live constantly doing rituals, which is the handling of the energies of the universe and Earth to send them to all of these places, with the intention of helping to build a way by which people can have strength in their heart to live and fight for their happiness.

In these types of situations that happen in life, it is very difficult to do something, as control is not in the hands of those who want to live in peace and harmony. Happiness and tranquillity are in the hands of those who, misconceiving the concept of life, take chaos and confusion to their people. These people are the ones that need much light to lead them out of their confusion and blindness which causes them to do harm. This is why the Masters, in a very constant way, do Love rituals directed specially at them, with the hope that their part of darkness can be illuminated with infinite Love.

In the same way, this energy helps to comfort each person that needs help, love or strength, because this received energy, handled and sent to us by the Masters, is a force from the Infinite; it is a force which will be deposited in our most subtle part, our heart.

I would like to explain in detail each one of the aspects of this energy that comes to our lives, but its power is so immense and fills us so much, that we can discover it only by feeling it through our own wisdom.

I know I have said this several times, but I did this because it is a reality. The Masters rely on something that goes beyond an explanation through spoken or written language. There are so many wonders which are around the life and mission of these beautiful beings that, through the mind, it would be impossible to understand. Because of this, I insist once that we open our hearts, to let us feel what we really are and give permission to ourselves to live in the reality that we take as fantasy. In this way, each one could be able to discover and know the mission of the Masters and, most importantly, to know oneself because that is the way of knowing everything else.

In the case of Master Sabadimel, he dedicates his life to his prayers, singing and rituals, and the places of power and strength of Earth to help us continue receiving our Mother energy from the Universe. He will continue in his Love fight until we remember and make again our way, finding ourselves again with those places that need us so much.

Thanks to the beloved Master Sabadimel, whom I call 'Guardian of the sacred places', our planet still has hope in each one of us, and we still have the strength to keep on, which in part is also thanks to our spirit of infinite force. But without doubt and in a definite way, if this force is still alive inside each one of us (even after so much unconsciousness, unbalance, pain and injustice there is in this world), we owe it to the Great Mission of Love given by these beings like Master Sabadimel in the name of the ultimate universal energy, with which they give hope to each inhabitant of Mother Earth, the hope that only Love can give.

It only remains for me to say that if Earth still has at least seventy power centres, the Masters will keep on fighting tirelessly so that each one of us can receive a part of the strength that the universe sends us. They want this for us each time we start a new day; it can be an opportunity to open our hearts to faith and Love in ourselves and all that is around us.

I am infinitely grateful to each one of them for all their Love…

Chapter 7

The Four Elements: Water, Earth, Wind and Fire

Nature and its wonders are without doubt our main guides and allies in our search for our path. However, much or almost everything has been forgotten regarding its importance and need in our life, physically and spiritually.

Our ancestors had a full and direct communication with the four elements, givers of life and wisdom. Because of this, their rituals and ceremonies were intended to honour each element, so that their strength and wisdom would be always present in each being and in their lives.

Their approach and communication with each element helped them to maintain the unity with the infinite and with all that was around them, enabling them to achieve so much in every area of their life. The awareness of their reality as sons of the universe was day after day preserved through the use and - most of all - the communication that they kept with Water, Earth, Wind and Fire.

For us, the present human beings, the communication and relationship with these four elements could seem absurd or impossible, above all because they are something with which we apparently have little or nothing in common. However, the reality is different, and it says that since the human being contains in his physical body each one of the elements as a fundamental part for its existence, it will be connected in a direct way with each one of them, as if it was one and the same family.

For most of us, the relationship and respect towards Water, Earth, Wind and Fire have been forgotten almost completely; this has taken us to ignore so much and to be so distant from our Mother Earth and her gifts. Communicating and living with the elements is a fundamental part for that light and guidance that we seek, and it is necessary to be able to find that wisdom within us that has been forgotten.

One of the first things that I had to learn from the Masters to be able to know more about myself and what is around me, was the conscious approach with each element so that then I would be able to understand their importance in the life of each human being.

At the beginning, I remember I did not understand why I had to be seated in front of the fire and put my hands close to it, to the point where it did not hurt me, with the purpose of feeling its warmth and all that which my body was feeling. However, I knew that I had to discover something in it and decided to let myself feel those sensations that seemed so relaxing.

Master Nintancito also asked me to play with each one of the elements, and to know what they meant for me. This was striking for me, as I thought in a sceptical way that it was not possible for them to give me something, because before that time I had used them I had never seen anything. But it turned out that there was nothing so far away from reality than those thoughts; little by little, I discovered that I had been completely blind, insensible and deaf to the natural elements and to the direct and real approach to them.

Wisdom of the Heart

My fascination to the wonders I found in Water, Earth, Wind and Fire was so big and powerful, that it helped me to know all that which up to that moment I did not understand. From the moment I discovered this wonderful energy, my mind was more flexible and my heart happier. Now I know that, thanks to their strength, I discovered part of mine, and this made it possible for me to be able to be on the level of closeness that I now have with the Masters.

Because of this I want to transmit to each person that reads this book, the importance of the closeness with our four elements, because each one of you will be able to discover each one of the wonders I talk about. With this you will get that inner closeness which is so necessary and essential for all those that seek happiness.

As I said before, the four elements are part of us, as our physical body is made up of Water, Earth, Wind and Fire, and it relies directly on them for its survival. Therefore, if these elements are so much related to our body, how is it possible that their closeness and understanding is almost zero for us? It would be logical for us to at least try to understand each one of them, being as they are so important for the correct functioning of our body.

Each element produces a unique and special energy that has an effect on both our physical and astral body. Our need to feel them is more than what we can realise; subconsciously our own body seeks this communication and makes us feel the need to be close to them.

A clear example of our wisdom compelling us to make this contact is Water. For all of us, to take a shower is a necessity, and when we make contact with the water, it gives us harmony and peace which makes us feel better. It gives us a sensation of being clean, not only on the physical level, but also on the astral level, as it gives us a sensation of liberation and closeness with this element.

If the tranquil sensation of taking a shower, which is made in a quick and subconscious way, is capable of helping us in such a relaxing way and makes us feel 'lighter', imagine the sensation of feeling and doing it with the conscious desire of achieving communication with Water? The best way to do this is to approach it as a child would do with something unknown, and leave behind all the concepts we might have had before about it, so that our body can feel its freshness and lightness. In that moment, we have to try to feel what water wants to give us, to be one with it and its language, to learn by ourselves the Infinite's message, through water. This will be a Love sensation that will help us to be sensible when dealing with our environment, and of course to understand a very important part of our being.

Let us not be afraid to say some words to something that we do not see as equal, let our actions and feelings transform into what they are, infinite and without limits. If we make this conscious approach when we are taking a shower, or in any other moment when we are near any of the elements, I can guarantee that the sensation will be that of encountering something that is already inside and has always been with us. Then, a feeling of peace and harmony will invade us, which will also help us in our daily relationships with our friends and family and with all that is around us.

The influence and presence of the four elements in our life is determined by our approach and understanding of what is infinite. There is no doubt about it, in order for us to understand each thing and discover the reality of whom we are and what is around us, we should be prepared.

The preparation for this approaching with ourselves, and the capability of being happy and sharing this happiness, are the necessary keys to achieving it; and for that, the four elements can help us much more than we believe.

We only need to give ten or twenty minutes of our day to the conscious approach with the elements, letting go of our prejudices and the 'fear' of discovering ourselves.

Here are some simple steps to help you become closer with the elements.

We need to sit comfortably on the floor or on a chair. The posture is not so important; what is more important is to be really comfortable in order to achieve harmony in our body.

We have to set in front of us each one of the four elements, represented in one of their many forms, for example:

Water: you can use a glass or clay container with enough water so that you can feel it in your hands.

Earth: you can use a NON-polished quartz crystal, a plant, a flower or anything that you consider represents the energy of the Earth element and that you can easily feel in your hands.

Wind: you can use any essence that you like, preferably incense, because through it you will see how the smoke takes forms of dances and its materialisation can be appreciated.

Fire: a candle is best because it is easy to handle, as you will have to concentrate on its strength and warmth, and also on its forms and colours.

After having these elements in front of us, and being seated in a comfortable position, we will initiate our ritual of closeness with them. First we should try to breathe in a calm and relaxed manner, without force, because the most important thing is to do it in accordance with our body, which will indicate the necessary rhythm to obtain harmony. When this occurs, we can start working with the first element.

It is not necessary to do everything in order. You can start with any element that is the most suitable for you; that is why we must pay attention to our body language and to our inner wisdom.

It is essential that this first phase of communication is done in this way, because our hands have a very important part to play in it. Through our energy receptive centres, located in the palms of our hands, we will achieve these first conscious approaches with our nature.

In the following step, we will rub our hands constantly until receiving the signal through a 'tickling' that will tell us that our receptive centres have been activated. It is then when we will take the first element. Let us suppose it would be Water. When taking this beautiful liquid in our hands, it should be done as if it is something unknown. It is necessary to forget our pre-conceived beliefs and to feel everything that, through the language of the sensations, will be given to us.

It is very important to merge our energy with the one of the water, and a way to do this will be to play with it. When we feel and see the water running in our hands, it will be leaving a message in each drop that only we can understand, and this will be transformed into balance and harmony, because this is its essence.

It does not matter how long we are in connection with each element. The coming together with the elements is something so great that many hours could go by without noticing it. Also, the willingness of the elements will be limitless and infinite.

Wisdom of the Heart

Afterwards, when switching to the next element (let us suppose it is the Earth element), we will initiate a journey of knowledge through the chosen element. Again, the important thing will be to take the element in our hands, because they will connect with the energy of each one. So we will take this element with the same purpose of looking for the message that wishes to be delivered to us.

If it is a flower, a crystal or soil, what is important is to merge with its energy, and this will be done through our energy centres, which will fill us with different emotions and feelings.

It is very important to touch the elements, not only with our hands, but by trying to go beyond matter, which is something that we human beings need to understand. But we have to start somewhere, and the closeness with the elements will help us understand that our hands, as any part of our body, have so many languages and ways to make us understand the 'Infinite Expression'. It is necessary for us to start letting go of our fear to touch and to try to see beyond.

With the element of Wind it is a little bit different, because to be able to get in its world you have to do it through observation. You can use incense, the scent of which will activate another part of your senses.

We have to observe the smoke coming out from the incense and concentrate on it, not through our mind, but experiencing the sensation of getting into a different world, to a place full of symbols and languages made for us. All of this will take us to move energies deposited inside of us, which will help us to free part of the emotions that have been affecting our lives.

We can try to only appreciate the incense smoke visually, or we can try to hold it in our hands, to start a little game with it and capture its energy. The forms that the incense smoke takes are so beautiful and incredible that, after discovering it, we will find it impossible to think that we did not appreciate it before and we did not recognise its beauty. This is something we see often but is hardly ever appreciated and cherished. However, it will give us something so beautiful that it will stay forever in our being. For sure I can tell you that this is more than a gaseous product or an uncompleted combustion, as some people define it.

Lastly, we have Fire which, as we know, is responsible for life just as the other elements are. If we have a candle we will be able to appreciate, through its little flame, endless extraordinary forms and colours that will have an effect on our being. The vision we have of it will help us to go inside its own energy to then merge with ours. Besides, we could do this connection through our hands so that they can feel its warmth and its language, without actually touching it.

It is so wonderful when we realise that we are a same being, that this strong and powerful energy that fire produces is the force of our Heart, of our blood, which is the intensity of Love in our being. But this is, without doubt, something that only each one of us can experiment and prove.

However, it is necessary to have patience, because generally human beings are impatient by inheritance, not by nature. If someone tells us that we will see and feel great things, we imagine a scene; if the reality does not match this idea, we immediately believe that it is not good or that maybe it is not for us.

It is important, as I said it at the beginning of this chapter, to leave all preconceived concepts behind; it is necessary to start a quest, knowing that what we will find will be totally unknown. For this we have to prepare ourselves with our Heart and not with our mind, which has learned all of the ideas and meanings known through books or experiences that are not ours. Let us leave all this and use only what is true: the Wisdom of our Hearts.

For this reason I will say it again: it is very difficult to explain the benefits that the closeness with the four elements can give us, but it depends on us to discover that they are infinite.

This is the reason why this is the last chapter of this book, because I know that many people will be asking: 'Is it possible to be aware of how real and wonderful our planet and our universe is?'

The answer is plain and simple: to feel and give Love to everything, not only to that which we see as equal. We have to let this Love be as it is, infinite and without limits. This can be achieved through the closeness with ourselves to then be able to achieve it towards the 'Infinite Expression'; for this to be possible, we have to activate the four forces of our creation, the force of our four elements: Water, Earth, Wind and Fire.

Let us remember that our body is much more than what we have thought and that it needs more than what we give to it. We need to activate it to its infinite capacity, let it enjoy of its own nature to let it get inside of us and us inside of it.

Let us let the wisdom of the past control our lives again; let us allow our spirit and our body to enjoy again its infinite capability to connect with what is sublime. Let us live again in harmony and communication with our brothers of Water, Earth Wind and Fire that are waiting to welcome us to the infinite reality and Happiness.

I remember with much happiness an experience that helped me to understand the importance of the four elements and their close relationship with human beings. I hope that this story helps to explain more clearly their function in our lives.

I was in a wonderful place in the United States of America, where there was a great reunion of different representatives of our Mother cultures from our planet. These were Masters that have kept their traditions and their way of life, with which they help to save what there is still of real wisdom.

For me, it was incredibly wonderful to be in a place so full of Magic, Wisdom, and Love, and see so many beings born on this Earth that still conserve what the present society has lost. It was a demonstration of showing what the sons of this Mother Earth can still do, to be what we really are. Many of these beautiful Native Masters are a real proof of what the human being once was, and they dedicate their lives to showing us the path, which we have abandoned.

The reason for this great reunion was to practise a beautiful ritual dedicated exclusively to all the sons of this Earth that live in ignorance of our greatness. This ritual took place throughout three days, and more than sixty Masters from different regions of the planet participated. Of course, my presence in it was not possible, as their preparation was totally infinite compared to my slow awakening. I had to stand about fifty meters away, in a prayer that would help me feel the energy that was going to be generated with this ritual.

What I experienced there was wonderful, and once again impossible to explain and assimilate. But I remember how the sky was illuminated in different coloured hues that I had never seen before. This scene was nothing compared to what I felt inside; the chants of the Masters in which they summoned Mother Earth and

Wisdom of the Heart

Father Sun, could be heard all the way to where I was.

I knew then that this ritual was done through the force of the four elements, which were present, and their force was called through the chants of the Masters. Chanting, they asked each element (Water, Earth, Wind and Fire) to take in their essence the force of infinite Love and deposit it into each son of the Earth. So then, the four elements are responsible for taking us to the strength of our spirit and creation.

In the last of the three rituals, I expressed to Nintancito my need to talk with the Masters that participated in the ritual. He told me that I only needed to get near them, which I did; I got near two Masters that were sitting on the ground in a position of connection with Earth and with themselves.

I asked for their permission to ask some questions and, with great sweetness, they agreed. One of them was a Native American and the other was from the Himalayas.

I asked them about the ritual and the reason for it, to which the Native American Master answered: 'Our universal body, as our body born in this Mother Earth, has been created from the four forces of the Father, transformed into Water, Earth, Wind and Fire. These forces connect us not only to Mother Earth but also with the Infinite. But you, the women and men from the present time, have forgotten this origin and its importance.

'You use our brothers of the Water without even thanking them; you step on Earth without even noticing its beauty; you breathe without being able to perceive the aroma of Air, and you receive Father Sun in the colours that decorate your environment without even being able to distinguish them. Because of this, we are asking our

145

brothers of the four elements to always cover and fill you with strength. Some day you will open your eyes to reality and will discover the brotherhood between Men, Women and Nature.

'They (making reference to our brothers, the elements) love you and each time that you make use of them, they make chants of joy with the hope of being heard by each one of you, as it was done by the grandparents of our grandparents. However, their calls are never recognised because they are disregarded by what has become the guidance of the contemporary men and women: the 'rational' mind that ignores all that it does not understand.

'Your world is beautiful and we are part of it, as we ALL come from the same source; and the invitation to live with them is always open to each one. May this ritual be to unite men and women with their reality...'

My amazement and admiration were infinite upon hearing these words. I did not know what to say. The Lama Master said: 'The men and women from the world have to understand that their reality is wonderful and full of happiness in each thing, as small as it looks. The guidance to this is found in each step, in each action, and can be achieved if you activate all of your strength through the four elements that are always waiting for you. The closeness with them has been there since conception; they are part of each moment, because this connection is present when you eat, when you work, or even in the daily events of life.

'These are opportunities to be close to something that is yourself, which can be found inside of each one of you. For it to be possible for our bodies to exist, there had to be a connection with each element and, with their magic and strength, they have given us life. Therefore, they are our creators and also our guides to what we really are. Who better than them to show us what they have created and kept alive? Life is what it is, thanks to their presence, and this presence is responsible for our creation.

'Opening the doors of Love and acknowledgment to our nature is what will take men and women from this millennium to recover the sacred part of their lives: the Love for the 'Infinite Expression'.

Their words were so full of Love, Truth and Wisdom that I could clearly understand the reason why these Masters perform one thousand, one hundred and seven rituals like this yearly, as well as the need for us to acknowledge the huge importance of the four elements. All of this, so that we, the men and women of the present time, can finally have a future full of Love, Peace and Happiness, that can take us to fulfil our Mission as beings of the Universe.

Epilogue

The Purpose of this Book

In each page of this book, all the Love energy from the Masters and the hope that it can reach to the hearts of everyone that reads it can be found. I wanted to give you something that, to the human mind, is impossible or simply considered as fantasy. I know it is not easy to defeat so many obstacles that prevent us from believing in all what is beautiful; however, my only purpose is to share a reality that has been forgotten for so long, with my deepest desire that it can be taken into consideration, at least as a possibility.

When the Masters, with such Love, asked me to share their mission, by way of speaking at lectures and conferences, it was not easy. First of all, I did not feel I was capable of doing it, because I considered that it was only worthy of someone with a much more superior spiritual preparation than mine.

I finally understood that I could do it, with the help and words of the Masters, as it was about speaking with the heart, from my experiences with each encounter and teaching. But then, I confronted another fear: the reaction of people. Even without knowing me, they would listen to things that even to me were hard to comprehend. Now, thanks to the support that the Masters have given me all this time, I have been able to overcome some of my fears and insecurities and, above all, my fear of people's

Flora Rocha

scepticism.

Over time, I have learned that we all, absolutely all, are the same being with the same needs, and that all we seek is happiness. I know that this message is not new; rather, it is part of us, and that it is only necessary to reach it and take it again in our lives.

It is not about convincing people. It is just about arousing, with memories, something that is already inside the Heart of each one: the Wisdom of our creation. Each experience captured here has to be, before taken as a reality, set to a test by the Heart, because it is the only one that can tell us the truth.

If your Heart, when reading this book, was able to feel something that felt like a memory, if for a moment it was able to live the experiences of these beautiful Masters, then the purpose for the publishing of this book has been fulfilled. Above all, the mission of the Masters has taken a step forward to the hearts of each one.

This book is just the first of many more. I was only able to write a small part of an infinite reality; however, I know it is enough for this first step towards the Wisdom of the Heart. As I said before, it is not about convincing anyone, but to discover that our world, our universe, and also our life, are full of wonders that we have missed, but that we still have time to discover and enjoy to the fullest extent. With this, we will achieve a closeness with our Masters and the Infinite.

I am infinitely grateful to the Masters and each person who, throughout these years, has been able to recognise their mission of being happy through the awakening of this Wisdom of their Hearts, and who have supported me at each step. I also excuse myself for my lack of experience in writing books. I have never done it before and I am not prepared for it, but you can be sure that it is done with all my Heart.

I want to finish by asking each person that reads this, to remember that, everywhere on this planet, a wonderful being is found, an angel that is by our side fighting, minute by minute, to guide us towards our mission of being happy. They have always given us their Love and strength with the purpose of making the connection of the universe with Earth possible without limits. Let us fight with the weapons of Love and Wisdom of our Hearts so that it can be...

Other Titles by
Mirage Publishing

A Prescription from The Love Doctor: How to find Love in 7 Easy Steps - Dr Joanne 'The Love Doctor' Coyle

Burnt: One Man's Inspiring Story of Survival - Ian Colquhoun

Cosmic Ordering Guide - Stephen Richards

Cosmic Ordering Connection - Stephen Richards

Cosmic Ordering: Chakra Clearing - Stephen Richards

Cosmic Ordering: Rapid Chakra Clearing – Stephen Richards

Cosmic Ordering: You can be Successful - Stephen Richards

Die Laughing: War Humour from WW1 to Present Day - George Korankye

Hidden Secrets: Attract Everything You Want! – Carl Nagel

Internet Dating King's Diaries: Life, Dating and Love – Clive Worth

Life Without Lottie: How I survived my Daughter's Gap Year - Fiona Fridd

Mrs Darley's Moon Mysteries: A Celebration of Moon Lore and Magic – Carole Carlton

Mrs Darley's Pagan Whispers: A Celebration of Pagan Festivals, Sacred Days, Spirituality and Traditions of the Year – Carole Carlton

Rebel Diet: They Don't Want You To Have It! – Emma James

The Hell of Allegiance: My Living Nightmare of being Gang Raped and Held for Ten days by the British Army – Charmaine Maeer with Stephen Richards

The Real Office: An Uncharacteristic Gesture of Magnanimity by Management Supremo Hilary Wilson-Savage - Hilary Wilson-Savage

The Tumbler: Kassa (Košice) – Auschwitz – Sweden - Israel - Azriel Feuerstein (Holocaust survivor)

Mirage Publishing Website:

www.miragepublishing.com

Submissions of Mind, Body & Spirit, Self Improvement, How To, Biography and Autobiography manuscripts welcomed from new authors.